Accounting Control
and
Organizational Behaviour

Accounting Control
and
Organizational Behaviour

DAVID OTLEY

*Department of Accounting and Finance,
University of Lancaster*

Heinemann Professional Publishing

Heinemann Professional Publishing Ltd,
Halley Court, Jordan Hill, Oxford OX2 8EJ

OXFORD   LONDON   MELBOURNE   AUCKLAND

First published 1987
Reprinted 1988
© David Otley 1987

British Library Cataloguing in Publication Data
Otley, David T.
Accounting control and organizational
behaviour.
1. Managerial accounting
I. Title
658.1'511   HF5635

ISBN 0 434 91480 0

Printed and bound in Great Britain by
Redwood Burn Limited, Trowbridge, Wiltshire

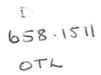

To Carolyn and Christopher

Contents

Introduction

It is now recognized that the successful design, implementation and operation of an accounting information system requires consideration of how the people who use it will react to the information that is provided. In addition, recent developments in accounting research are confirming what practising accountants already suspected, namely, that there is no single, best design for an accounting information system, but that it must be carefully tailored to match the environmental and organizational context in which it will be used.

However, most management accounting textbooks concentrate solely on the technical aspects of information systems design, and tend to assume that the systems they specify will be universally applicable. In this book, the accounting control process is set firmly into its organizational context with an emphasis on those human, motivational and organizational aspects of accounting that are essential to the successful operation of a real-world system.

Most importantly, it is recognized that the way in which accounting information is used by line managers is crucial in determining how effective the system will be in controlling performance. The accounting control system is but part of a wider system of management control, and its interconnections with other techniques of management control must be considered at the design stage.

Thus, this book goes beyond the material usually included in traditional management accounting texts and provides both managers and management accountants with a simple guide to the major issues involved in developing and using accounting systems for management control. Attention is focused particularly on budgetary control systems because these form the basis for management control in most organizations of any size. However, relevant information on the behavioural and organizational aspects of budgeting is not readily accessible, so this book is an attempt to distil the major research findings now available into a compact and readable form. The final part contains a checklist of questions that can be used to conduct a thorough review of an organization's management accounting practices.

Finally, the book will be of use to students of management accounting, both those on degree courses and those taking the final examinations of the Chartered Institute of Management Accountants and other accounting bodies, as the importance of the material included is becoming recognized and incorporated into the examination syllabuses.

I am grateful to the members of the Management Control Association who have been a constant source of inspiration, encouragement and constructive criticism during the period over which this book was written; also to the managers in many organizations who have freely given their time to help with the research work on which this book is based.

David Otley
October 1986

PART ONE

Theory

· I ·

Accounting for management control

A modern business organization is an extremely complex entity. Its continued existence depends upon its matching the needs of a large number of people including customers, suppliers, employees and providers of finance. It employs people with many different skills and a variety of expertise, often working in widely scattered locations. Raw materials and other goods and services are obtained from other organizations on a world-wide basis. The products it manufactures are often of considerable technical sophistication and great variety, and may be distributed and sold around the globe. People, machines and money are combined together to produce goods and services on a scale that is unique to the present age.

It is easy to take the existence of such organizations for granted, but it is really quite remarkable that enterprises on such a scale can not only exist and survive, but can also grow and prosper over periods of many years. Of course, a business enterprise is not always successful. Many small firms fail to develop into larger ones and frequently fail to survive at all. Even well established organizations can fail to adapt to trends in consumer demand or technological changes and may be forced to withdraw from whole areas of activity with consequential problems for their employees, suppliers and even customers. Yet, even when faced with such problems on a massive scale, the organization usually survives, albeit in a more or less drastically amended form. How is it that an activity of such obvious complexity can be coordinated and controlled so that it continues to meet the needs of those having an interest in it?

The major responsibility for the control of a business enterprise rests with its directors and managers. Large organizations typically have several tiers of management arranged in a hierarchy. The major duty of these managers is to guide, coordinate and control those who actually perform the tasks necessary for organizational survival. Indeed, responsibility for organizational control is such a central feature of managerial work that writers such as Stafford Beer have described management as 'the profession of control'.

This responsibility for control can be effected in a variety of ways. At the lowest level in the hierarchy direct personal supervision and 'man-management' is of paramount importance. However, at more senior levels, although personal contact is still of great importance, it is not sufficient for effective control. The manager necessarily has to rely upon less direct means of control, especially where operations are carried out by large numbers of people in geographically dispersed locations. In these circumstances formal management information systems become important.

Information has been aptly described as the cement that binds an organization together. Without the regular flow of relevant information for coordination and control, the organization would fall apart. Much information used by managers is obtained informally, sometimes accidentally; some is speculative and qualitative in nature. But the hard core of management information is provided by formal systems that are consciously designed to provide managers with the vital information they need. A major part of this formal information is expressed in financial terms and is channelled through the management accounting system.

The management accounting system is therefore a central feature of the management control system, and provides essential information for the overall control of the enterprise. Its most noticeable characteristic is that much of the information it conveys is expressed in terms of money. This focus on the financial dimension of organizational activity is often misunderstood. It does not occur because the business is viewed as being solely about making money, although it must be admitted that the generation of surplus funds is a necessary condition for survival. Rather, it occurs because money provides a convenient common language in which the results of a wide variety of activities can be expressed and summarized. Money is the language of business mainly because there is no other way yet discovered by which the results of dissimilar activities can be measured and aggregated together in common terms.

This perspective on the use of accounting information as a means of management control is not intended to play down the role of financial information for other purposes. The function of financial management is as vital to the well-being of the enterprise as the other major business functions such as marketing, production or personnel. Yet its status is that of being just one function of the many functions that are necessary for an organization to be effective. Financial accounting reports, as well as being a legal requirement, are influential in projecting an image of the organization to the providers of capital, and the constraints imposed by the capital market will be felt by all parts of the organization. Information for financial management is essential for the effective operation of the finance function. Nevertheless, the central theme of this book is the provision of accounting information as an aid to management control and the ways in which the managerial use of this information can influence overall organizational behaviour.

There is little doubt that accounting information can be highly influential in affecting what managers actually do. There is a great deal of evidence available to support the contention that giving managers a financial target, and making it clear that their performance will be evaluated in relation to that target, can be a most effective means of motivation. Unfortunately, the same evidence also suggests that managers may well try to meet their target by taking actions that are not in the best interests of their organization (see Chapters 4 and 5). For example, in the quest to keep within a cost target, product quality may suffer, expenditures on items having a long-term benefit (such as repairs and maintenance) may be cut, stock levels may be adversely affected and cooperation with other departments may be jeopardized. The art of using accounting information for effective control is still not fully understood, but we will be exploring many of its aspects in subsequent chapters of this book.

Basic issues in management control

In the design of a management control system there are three basic questions that need to be answered. However there are no definitive answers to these questions, and the operation of a management control system can be seen as the continual development of new solutions to the same fundamental problems. The three questions are:

1 What are the dimensions of 'good' performance that the organization is seeking to encourage?
2 How are appropriate standards of performance to be set, both for the whole organization and for its segments?
3 What rewards (penalties) are to be associated with the achievement (non-achievement) of performance targets?

Dimensions of good performance

The first question is the most fundamental and also the most difficult to answer. At the level of the overall organization there is not usually a single objective that completely defines what 'good' performance should be. Even if profitability is taken as a major objective, questions are raised such as the relative emphasis on short-term as against long-term profit, how profitability should be measured (e.g. in relation to capital employed, etc.), and its relationship with growth and liquidity. More crucially, how to obtain good profitability in a complex, competitive and uncertain environment is not a well-understood process. Thus subsidiary dimensions of good performance do not necessarily follow by a process of logical deduction from an overall goal, even where one exists.

Next, these overall goals have to be decomposed into various subsidiary goals relating to such matters as product range, product quality, customer service, market segmentation and so on. Further goals need to be developed for the various parts of the organization and the business functions such as production, marketing and research and development. Thus the dimensions of good performance that are defined for a segment of the organization are likely to be multiple and partially conflicting (e.g. product quality v product cost; quantity sold v price obtained).

Finally, although some aspects of good performance can be quantified (e.g. sales targets, cost budgets), many other aspects are less quantifiable (e.g. product image, employee morale) although no less important. Even where a goal is quantifiable, the means of achieving it may not be well understood. Thus, any programme of action designed to achieve these goals is open to discussion and debate concerning its likely effectiveness. Discussion of means (such as plans, budgets and action programmes) is likely to be used as a means of amending ends even when these are not items ostensibly under consideration.

Thus the question of how good performance is defined is one that is subject to continual debate and amendment within an organization. At any one time the dimensions being emphasized are likely to be multiple, partially conflicting and often ambiguous. To the extent that means-end relationships are not fully understood, plans designed to achieve those goals are also debatable in terms of their likely effectiveness.

Setting performance standards

The second question is closely related to the first. Even if an adequate set of performance dimensions can be obtained, appropriate standards of performance need to be set. Here, there is an immediate conflict between what is desirable and what is attainable, with both being subject to considerable ambiguity. Although more profit may be preferred to less, the situation is less clear-cut when subsidiary objectives are considered. For example, should product quality be improved or costs cut? The degree to which an objective can be attained is also difficult to predict. This second problem is compounded by the fact that the people in the best position to make such judgements about the feasibility of proposed targets are often managers who will ultimately be held accountable for meeting the standard that is set. In such circumstances there is an obvious motivation for managers to be less than totally candid in the information they give.

This conflict between what is desirable and what is attainable reverberates up and down the organization, with senior managers tending to emphasize overall desirability and lower level managers being more concerned with feasibility. It affects matters such as planning procedures (top-down v bottom-up), participation in decision-making (participation, consultation or neither) and organizational design (span of control v number of hierarchical levels), as well as the design of management information systems. The process of budget-setting is absolutely dependent upon quantitative standards of performance being available, and the whole question of performance standards will be considered at length in later chapters.

Linking rewards with performance

The final question is concerned with the association of reward structures with performance targets. It is all very well to set quantitative performance targets for managers, but they will be effective only to the extent that the manager is motivated to achieve the target set. This requires the establishment of mechanisms linking target achievement to valued, although not necessarily financial, rewards. These mechanisms can take a variety of forms, ranging from the encouragement of cohesive peer groups where members assist and encourage each other in achieving targets (characteristic of Japanese styles of management) to the explicit linking of substantial monetary rewards to target attainment (most prevalent at senior management levels in the USA, but also inherent in all incentive payment schemes).

There is no doubt that incentives can be devised that will encourage managers to achieve, or at least report, a high degree of target attainment, but the means by which this is attained is often not what was intended or desired. In particular, such schemes emphasize the independence of each organizational unit from other units in the firm, and encourage a high level of competition between managers that may be harmful where cooperation is necessary for successful performance. In addition, these schemes may encourage the bias and manipulation of accounting information, so that senior managers become increasingly misinformed about what is actually happening, while believing that all is well.

A contingent approach

As a management control system continues in use, the tentative answers initially assumed to each of these questions tend to be adapted in the light of experience and changing circumstances. Not only do definitive answers to the questions not exist, even tentative answers are likely to be different for different organizations operating in different circumstances. The recognition of the existence of these inherent differences has led to the development of the so-called 'contingency theory' of management accounting. The fundamental basis of contingency theory is that the most appropriate control system for an organization depends upon certain contingent variables; that is, the system must be matched with circumstances. General, all-purpose systems are unlikely to be uniformly successful as the management control system requires to be tailored to fit the specific circumstances of the organization for which it is intended.

The major contingent variables that have been suggested to date are the nature of the environment in which the organization is set, the types of task it undertakes and the technology it utilizes, the organizational structure it has adopted and the strategy it is attempting to pursue. It is also evident that the culture in which the organization operates, both in terms of national characteristics and the internal organizational culture, will have an important impact.

Aspects of the environment that have been considered important include its uncertainty, complexity, rate of change, hostility and the degree of competitiveness it displays. Technology has been characterized by its complexity and its degree of predictability in producing desired results. Consideration of the effect of organizational structure on management information systems design has been mainly concerned with matching task interdependence with the structure imposed upon it. Finally, corporate strategy is of evident importance in defining appropriate goals and encouraging an appropriate cultural climate to design reward systems that will produce the desired levels of motivation.

Empirical studies of management control systems based on the contingency framework have not yet been very successful in providing a basis for prescription, but the subject is only at a rudimentary stage of development and holds considerable promise for the future. For the moment, the design of management control systems remains more of an art than a science, with organizations learning from their mistakes as they adapt and amend their systems. Accounting systems are only one part of an overall management control system, but they are a central and vitally important one. We will therefore consider the specific role of accounting information in the management control process more fully in the next section.

Types of control

The accounting information system provides an aid to managers attempting to control a set of activities for which they are being held responsible. It focuses primarily on those aspects of managerial performance that can be measured and quantified in financial terms, and is thus most appropriate for use at senior management levels where direct personal controls are no longer adequate. Accounting controls are typically of relatively less importance at junior levels and where purely physical measures of performance can be utilized. They are thus of most significance in large, diversified organizations where financial information provides the only feasible mechanism for summarizing the overall performance of the total organization.

Central to the appropriate use of accounting information as a means of control is the degree of knowledge of means-end relationships possessed by managers concerning the process they are managing. Sometimes the process is sufficiently well-understood for senior managers to give specific and detailed instructions about exactly what should be done so that desired objectives are achieved. Such instructions have been described as *behaviour* controls (Ouchi, 1979) as they prescribe the behaviour required of the subordinate manger. The use of such controls is most common at the lower levels of organizations where the tasks to be undertaken by employees are well-understood and a bureaucratic form of organization appropriate. Examples would include routine clerical work and the operation of a mass production line.

However, in many circumstances managers do not possess the detailed knowledge necessary to implement behaviour controls, and have to resort to the use of *output* controls. That is, senior managers specify the results that are to be achieved, but the detailed means by which these are achieved is left to the discretion and specialized knowledge of the subordinate. Thus, in a diversified company, divisional managers may be set profit or return on investment targets but are allowed to try to achieve them in any way that they see fit.

Unfortunately, in some circumstances it is not possible to specify even overall output targets in financial terms. For example, how can the performance of headquarter service departments such as the legal department be measured? Or what financial targets can be set for a research and development department in the short term? Here only *input* controls can be used. These specify the resources that are allocated to the department and which may be used during the accounting period, but no attempt is made to specify required outputs in financial terms.

Methods of accounting control include all of these categories. For example, accounting controls are almost always input controls as they measure the use made of scarce resources in financial terms. They become output controls when the results of the activity are measured and valued in the same way, as in the construction of profit budgets for profit centres. They may also be used as behaviour controls to the extent that the plan they reflect and the amount allocated to each account heading constrains a manager to obtain the desired results in a pre-determined manner, rather than allowing greater freedom of choice. What is important is that the type of accounting control operated is consistent with the underlying circumstances of the operation being controlled. For example, attempting to operate behaviour controls when senior management do not have the knowledge necessary to specify appropriate managerial behaviour is doomed to failure.

In most organizations, the use of accounting information for management control is closely connected with the operation of a system of budgetary control. A budget can be defined as the quantitative expression in financial terms of the expected results of a plan of action. The construction and use of a system of budgetary control requires that the three basic questions posed in the previous section be answered.

In a budget, the dimensions of what is regarded as 'good' or 'acceptable' performance are spelt out in precise terms. This is true even for an input budget, as might be produced for a cost centre, in that it specifies required behaviour. However it is much more evident in a budget for a profit centre, which relates inputs to outputs. Here expected costs and revenues are estimated, resulting in an overall figure of profit or return on capital employed. The budget figure also represents a standard of performance that is required to be obtained, whether this is arrived at by participation, consultation or imposition from above. Finally, a reward structure is implicit in the system of accountability that is associated with the budget system for, at the end of the day, managers will be held accountable for their performance in relation to the budget standard.

Conclusions

It is therefore apparent that, in this whole process of budgetary control, the most important feature is not the technical construction of the budget itself (vital though this is) but rather the way in which senior management use the budget information as a means of influencing the behaviour of their subordinates. Because the budget inevitably does not capture all the aspects of managerial activity that need to be monitored and controlled, it is all too easy to over-emphasize those aspects that can be quantified at the expense of those which cannot. In particular, this can lead to an emphasis on short-term financial results to the detriment of longer-term and more strategic results.

The design of an effective system of accounting for management control requires a careful matching of the capabilities of the accounting system with the requirements of the organization. Not only must the technical design of the system be adequate for the demands made of it, but the way in which it is used by senior managers must also be appropriate. The careful interweaving of accounting and non-accounting methods of control to encourage desirable patterns of managerial behaviour is a centrally important skill that a senior manager must acquire. The remainder of this book is devoted to exploring some of the major aspects involved in developing this skill.

· 2 ·

Control systems
and human behaviour

The word 'control' is probably one of the most ill-defined in the English language, having a wide range of connotations, ranging from 'manipulate' through 'inspect' to 'prohibit'. Within this variety, however, there are two main themes. First, there is the idea of control as domination, where one person imposes his/her will upon others by the exercise of power or authority. Second, there is the idea of control that emphasizes the gathering of information to regulate and monitor activities to ensure that some desired outcome is obtained, or a desired state of affairs maintained. In a more general sense, control is concerned with the processes by which a system adapts its internal behaviour in response to changes in its external environment. However defined, control processes are a central part of human activity, regardless of whether they are viewed from an individual, organizational or societal perspective.

Management control systems

Indeed, this is one of the main problems in studying the operation of management control systems within business organizations, for the exercise of control is not confined solely to those people termed 'managers'. Each person in the organization is engaged in behaviour that is designed to achieve certain desired outcomes, whether for him/her or for others. Often this exercise of control is quite natural or subconscious, and certainly does not rely on formal mechanisms of control. Neither is its direction of operation only from the top to the bottom of the organizational hierarchy. Subordinates attempt to control the behaviour of their superiors, often very successfully, just as much as their superiors attempt to control them. Participants at all levels in organizations have sources of power available to them which they can use to control the behaviour of others.

A major source of such power lies in the access to, and use of, information. It is often the person who actually performs a particular task who is best informed about what is going on, and what is feasible in the future. In one factory it was noted that the single person most vital to its efficient running was an elderly storekeeper whose main expertise was that he knew where things could be found!

However, the control exercised by individuals is most evidently concerned with the attainment of their own aims and objectives. More explicit and formal control systems are required to ensure that overall organizational goals and objectives are pursued and achieved. This point of view is reflected in a definition of a mangement control system advanced by Lowe (1970):

> A system of organizational information seeking and gathering, accountability and feedback designed to ensure that the enterprise adapts to changes in its substantive environment and that the work behaviour of its employees is measured by reference to a set of operational subgoals (which conform with overall objectives) so that the discrepancy between the two can be reconciled and corrected for.

A management control system (MCS) can therefore be seen as a set of control mechanisms designed to help organizations regulate themselves, although it must be noted that the term MCS is understood differently by different writers. Another useful approach to its definition has been put forward by Machin (1983) who took the three words 'management', 'control' and system' as progressively defining a set of activities of interest. Thus, *management* is a subset of all the activities that go on in an organization, *control* is a subset of the total range of management activity and *systems* is the subset of organizational systems that includes only formal, systematically developed, data-handling systems.

Such a definition ties in closely with Anthony's (1965) classic definition of management control as 'the process by which managers assure that resources are obtained and used effectively and efficiently in the accomplishment of the organization's objectives'. Anthony has himself pioneered teaching and research into the use of accounting systems for management control, although he believes that social psychology rather than economics forms the basic source discipline on which management control rests. Machin quite clearly exposes the dilemma between the technical accounting system and the behavioural consequences of control that Anthony's framework contains, and maintains that it was inevitable that the focus of the study of MCSs would swing away from the purely technical accounting aspects of control.

Thus, a useful management control system cannot confine itself solely to accounting measures of performance, important as these undoubtedly are. It has also to be concerned with those areas of performance that cannot be measured in precise, quantitative terms according to a regular schedule. For example, market share and competitive position, employee commitment and morale, and the state of research and development work into new products are all vitally important to the continued well-being of the enterprise, but cannot be captured by accounting numbers alone. Even when accounting information can be used, it is the response of individual people to that information that is crucial to its effectiveness in bringing about overall organizational control. Management control is therefore as much to do with influencing human behaviour as it is to do with the technical design of information systems.

A model of the control process

It is helpful at this stage to look more deeply at what the 'control' of a process involves. If we consider the process being controlled in general terms as a black box which converts inputs into outputs, but whose internal operations are unknown to us, the control process can be shown diagrammatically as in Figure 1. There are four necessary conditions that must be satisfied before the process can be said to be controlled (Otley and Berry, 1980). These are:

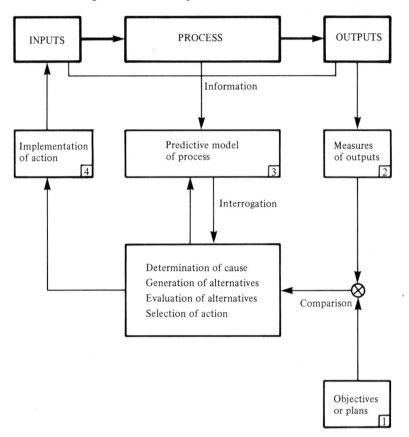

Figure 1 *A model of a controlled process*

1 Objectives must exist, for without an aim or purpose control has no meaning.
2 The output of the process must be capable of being measured in the same terms as the objectives being pursued. This allows a comparison to be made between desired and actual attainment of objectives.
3 A predictive model of the process being controlled must exist. This enables the cause of failure to meet an objective to be ascertained and, even more importantly, the consequences of proposed alternative corrective actions to be evaluated.
4 The capability must exist to take effective corrective action that will reduce the deviation of actual performance from that which is desired.

It is helpful to apply this model of control to a simple business controlled by its owner. The first condition indicates that there must be some objective for the business, which might be the generation of profit for the owner. However, the situation is more complex than such an apparently simple objective may imply. For example, to what extent is profit this year to be preferred to profit next year, or in subsequent years? Should immediate profit be sacrificed in order to obtain a competitive advantage? Although the owner may be willing to give up immediate returns in exchange for future pay-offs, there is likely to be a minimum level of liquidity required to ensure current survival, as the financial resources of the business are limited.

Thus, a more sophisticated and complete objective might be the maximization of the net present value (NPV) of future cash flows, subject to a liquidity constraint. But to follow such an objective implies the existence of a very high level of predictive ability in forecasting the effect of current decisions on future cash flows. To make such an objective operational will usually require a set of surrogate goals to be devised (e.g. production and sales targets, profit margins, other financial targets, market share targets etc.) that are measurable immediately in reasonably objective terms. Thus, in practice, operational goals are multiple and often partially conflicting.

The second condition for control requires that actual performance can be measured in terms of the dimensions defined by the selected objectives. This indicates a second problem with the NPV objective suggested above. It is not possible to quantify how well it has been achieved until all the cash flows have materialized; but by that time it is too late to implement any effective control actions. Control can only be effectively exercised on the basis of some surrogate goals where actual achievement can be measured at the end of a given time period. This is the strength of accounting income measures, which have been devised to cope with precisely this problem of measuring outcomes of an on-going process at regular intervals. Thus profits, year-end cash balances and market positions are feasible control objectives, even if they are only loosely related to more complete and fundamental long-term objectives.

The third condition for control is perhaps the most important to be borne in mind by the designer of a management control system.

Control can be exercised only if the controller has a predictive model of the process being controlled. Such a model has to be capable of predicting, with reasonable accuracy, both the causes of deviations from desired objectives and the likely effects of potential control actions. When an objective is not being achieved, it is first necessary to discover the reasons why actual performance has fallen short of what was required. This may be self-evident, as when particular subsidiary targets have not been met, or it may require a detailed investigation to be mounted: in both cases a model capable of predicting what might have happened in different circumstances is required. Such a predictive model may exist only in the mind of the manager, although in large and more complex organizations attempts are often made to make it explicit, perhaps in the form of a computerized corporate model.

More importantly, the same model is required to predict the likely outcomes of possible control actions. For example, the owner of our small business may be considering altering the quality of the product, or changing its price. To take a rational decision on such matters it is necessary to be able to predict, to some reasonable degree of accuracy, the likely outcomes of the decision in terms of its effects on the attainment of objectives. If they are unable to make such predictions, they cannot make a rational choice and the business is essentially out of control.

Finally, a controlled process requires the ability to implement an effective control action. It is all very well to decide that the problems of the business would be solved by a substantial cash injection, but unless it is possible to find a willing lender no effective action can be taken, and collapse is probable. Thus the ability to implement effective control actions is the final necessary condition for control.

This model of control is recursive, in that it may be applied at any level of analysis. For example, it may be used by an individual controlling a mechanical process (e.g. driving a car), by a group controlling a social process (e.g. running a club), or by an organization running a business that combines both technical and social processes. Looking at control in this way immediately indicates one major problem in the design of MCSs. Because management control is concerned with the control of human behaviour, the process being controlled involves many different people. Each of these people can be viewed as a self-controlling system pursuing its own individual objectives. When the organization takes a control action, the effect is difficult to predict because it is necessary to forecast all the individual adaptations that will be made in response to this action, and also their consequent interactions. It is therefore unlikely that a practical MCS will have an adequate predictive model within it able to fully evaluate the effects of alternative control actions.

The implications for accounting are clear enough. An accounting or financial model of an organization is only partial, and contains insufficient information for overall organizational control. However, the accounting model is important and necessary, even though it is insufficient. It is necessary because it relates to a relevant environment, but it is insufficient because it is only partial and does not fully take into account other relevant environments. This is not to say that development and improvement cannot take place. Indeed, the provision of appropriate information to allow prediction of a wider range of relevant outcomes is perhaps the most important extension of an organization's accounting system that can be envisaged.

Accountants possess a good basis, perhaps the only basis, for the development of an integrated management control and information system, provided they extend their thinking in the application of their most powerful tool, accounting method (Lowe, 1970). This implies that accountants must be prepared to include within their remit the collection of information concerning a far wider range of variables than has traditionally been the case. In particular, they need to be concerned with the prior activity of planning and the subsequent activity of performance appraisal as parts of the overall process of control.

Planning and control

It is conventional to separate the processes of planning and control, defining planning as the setting of objectives and the outlining of a defined set of actions needed to attain them, and control as ensuring that these plans are implemented and the objectives achieved. But applying the control model developed in the previous section indicates that not only does control require plans, but also that the process of planning is itself a *control* process.

Why do we plan? A simple answer to this question is that in planning we seek to take current decisions in such a way as to ensure that some future desired state comes into being. In this sense, planning has been defined as future control (Wildavsky, 1975). Notice that the essence of planning is that we take action *now* in order to gain some expected future benefit. If the result of planning is that the actions we take are no different to those that would have been taken before the planning exercise was undertaken, then planning has served no useful purpose (except, perhaps, to convince us more strongly that our present course of action is correct).

This analysis immediately suggests two possible reasons for not planning, or for not implementing plans. First, we may not have sufficient confidence in our predictions to risk making a current sacrifice to obtain expected future benefits. The future involves uncertainty and we may decide that, on balance, a more certain return now is preferable to a larger, but less certain, return in the future. That is, our *risk* preference is such that the current benefit is preferred to the more risky future benefit. Second, we may prefer a benefit now to even a certain future benefit. That is, our *time* preference is such that the current benefit is sought, despite the realization that an improved benefit would be obtained in the future. In practice, the combination of risk and time preferences may explain the tendency for corporate plans to remain on the shelf between neatly bound covers rather than being implemented.

However, it is worthwhile to look more closely at the process of planning, using the model of control outlined in Figure 1. By its very nature, planning requires a predictive model capable of forecasting the likely outcomes of various alternative courses of action. Further, the predicted outcomes of these plans will be compared with the various success criteria or objectives developed by the organization, and the plan yielding the best results selected. If no plan is thought to give satisfactory results, then re-planning takes place until a more acceptable alternative is produced. Finally, to be effective, the decisions implied by the plan must be implemented. Thus, three of the four necessary conditions for control are also necessary conditions for planning. That is:

1 Objectives must exist.
2 There must be an adequate predictive model.
3 There must be the ability to act.

But, whereas control is error-led (i.e. the control process is instigated by feeding back information on an observed difference between actual and desired results), the planning process is instigated by the realization that expected results are likely to deviate from those desired. That is, the control process begins by measuring actual performance, whereas the planning process begins by predicting expected performance. But otherwise, planning and control are entirely similar processes that operate in identical ways. In technical terms, the control process we have described here is termed (negative) *feedback* control, because the observed error is fed back into the process to instigate action to cause its reduction. By contrast, planning can be described as *feedforward* or anticipatory control, because it is only an expected error that is used to stimulate the control process.

Thus planning is an important form of control. The main objection to the use of feedback control is that errors are allowed to occur before they are corrected, and the process is therefore often in a less than desirable state. Feedforward control attempts to overcome this problem by predicting potential errors in advance and taking corrective actions designed to prevent them from occurring. Such prediction evidently requires the use of predictive model that is sufficiently accurate to ensure that the control action taken will improve the situation rather than causing it to deteriorate further.

Unfortunately, our models of organizational behaviour are generally rather weak, and in some circumstances planning may be counter-productive because it suggests taking remedial action to avoid situations that would not, in fact, have occurred. Where predictive ability is absent, it is often replaced by assertion and belief. Action may thus be based on beliefs that prove to be unwarranted. Improvement of control in such circumstances is possible only by testing the validity of the underlying assumptions and coming to a better understanding of the reality of the situation being faced.

Such an improvement of the predictive models used by an organization is part of the more general process of organizational learning, and can only occur by the intelligent analysis of past actions in a spirit of learning from mistakes rather than using the process to attach blame. That is, performance appraisal is a vital means of improving the future performance of an organization, and is a central part of the control process itself.

Performance appraisal

We have argued that the management control process is essentially concerned with encouraging individuals within an organization to alter their behaviour so that the overall aims of the organization are effectively and efficiently attained. This not only requires that individuals know exactly what is expected of them, but also that they are motivated to achieve these expectations. Both aspects of this process are problematic.

The first requires that the overall goals and plans of the organization are broken down into subgoals and operational plans for the separate parts. In practice, this becomes successively more difficult at each stage in the process. For example, although an overall profit goal might be decomposed into profit goals for parts of the organization, this can become a meaningless exercise if carried too far. Some functional departments, such as the legal and finance departments, give services that are difficult to value in monetary terms, and are usually treated as cost centres in which only resource inputs are valued. Even major line responsibilities, such as production and marketing, may not be sensibly separable in a way that allows separate profit targets to be set for each part. A major car company perceived its main problems to be in the marketing area because its transfer pricing policy was such as to show the production departments to be making a profit while concentrating all losses into the marketing department accounts. In fact, cost control was as much a problem as marketing. But, even when explicit targets can be set for a subunit, a second difficulty arises in motivating the managers concerned to meet the targets set. This is essentially a behavioural rather than a technical problem, and is dealt with primarily by a system of performance appraisal.

In its simplest form, performance appraisal works as a simple feedback control system. Managers are set performance targets specified in quantitative terms and, at the end of a given period of time, are held accountable for the attainment of the targets by their superiors. Evidently this requires both that appropriate standards of performance are set initially and also that an accurate means of recording actual results exists. It can be quite difficult to achieve such a state of affairs, and the practical problems of using accounting information in performance appraisal are dealt with more fully in Chapter 5.

For the present, it is important to note that such *ex post* evaluation is not usually sufficient for effective control, because the system responds only after deviations have occurred. A better system would act before actual performance moved away from target. In practice, the very fact that managers know in advance that they are going to be held accountable for their subsequent performance is likely to motivate them to take actions to avoid the possibility of future criticism. However, it is possible that they will merely alter the information that they report. This process, sometimes known as information inductance (Prakash and Rappaport, 1977), is essentially an individual control device that acts to prevent organizational controls operating.

Systems of performance appraisal, conducted by such devices as accountability meetings, are sufficiently powerful methods of managerial motivation that we have to be concerned less about whether they are effective in motivating desirable managerial behaviour than whether they are *too* effective in motivating inappropriate behaviour. For if managers are set targets that are not totally valid, and meeting these targets is unduly stressed by senior managers, they may be tempted to achieve them in ways other than those intended. That is, if mangers are judged by output controls, they may indulge in undesirable behaviour in order to produce measures of output that are in accord with the standards set for them to achieve.

One common example of such behaviour is where divisional managers are set return on investment (RoI) targets. Suppose a manager is set an RoI target of 15 per cent and has two investment opportunities available, which are expected to yield 10 and 20 per cent respectively. His/her attitude towards these opportunities may well depend upon the average RoI currently being earned, rather than the cost of capital to the company. Thus, if his/her current RoI is less than 10 per cent, the manager may wish to take on both projects, as each would increase the average RoI. Conversely, if the current RoI is in excess of 20 per cent, the manager may not wish to take on either project. However, from an overall company viewpoint, the manager should take on those projects with a projected return in excess of the company's cost of capital (which might rationally be assumed to be 15 per cent in this case). In this way a manager may attempt to meet what seems a perfectly sensible performance target in a way that is undesirable from an overall point of view.

Nevertheless the performance appraisal system is probably the most important means of regular, formal control operated in many organizations. Its particular virtue is that it allows senior managers to specify targets and goals for each subordinate manager in such a way as to balance quantitative and qualitative factors, short- and long-term time horizons, and current and future needs. Accounting information forms an important part of the appraisal process, but appraisal uses a wider array of sources of information than just those derived from accounting data. For a senior manager, the crucial art in performance appraisal lies in balancing the emphasis placed on accounting information with that placed on other measures of performance (Hopwood, 1972). There is also some evidence that the nature of this balance depends upon contingent factors in the situation itself, such as the degree of uncertainty involved in task completion. The more uncertain the task, the less emphasis can sensibly be placed on accounting measures of performance (Hirst, 1981). In the next and final section of this chapter, we shall briefly consider some of the non-accounting based means of control used in organizations.

Organizational control systems

All organizations use a wide range of controls designed to influence the behaviour of their employees. These controls range from bureaucratic rules and procedures which directly circumscribe employee behaviour, through formally designed management information and control systems, to the promulgation of various aspects of organizational culture and ethos that impinge less obviously, yet often very powerfully, on individual behaviour. Social controls, based on shared norms and values, affect behaviour as much as, if not more than, the more formal input, output and behaviour controls inherent in the formal control systems.

At the simplest level, rules and regulations can provide a very effective means of control if desirable behaviour patterns can be specified in detail. This state of affairs is most common at the lowest hierarchical levels, although even there rules can never provide all the control required. For example, the use of time clocks provides a means of monitoring whether employees turn up on time and are present in the workplace during the working day. At more senior levels clocking-in is not usually required, but a similar result is obtained by the use of social controls. Persistent late arrival may be informally noted and offenders have it brought to their attention that their progress within the organization may be adversely affected if their behaviour continues.

In some organizations there may be rules about such apparently peripheral matters as dress and speech. For example, some professional accounting firms set out detailed rules for articled clerks in their manuals of audit procedures regarding matters such as dress (suit, white collar, tie, etc.), and their attendance and demeanour on clients' premises. Such specific rules have the virtue of being easily enforced, but are effective only to the extent that the prescribed behaviour actually leads to desired outcomes. In most cases however such behaviour is at best a necessary condition for good performance, but is certainly not a sufficient condition (e.g. a worker may turn up on time, but still not perform his/her job effectively). In other cases the rule may not even be necessary, and may be flouted while highly effective performance is delivered. I can still vividly recollect a company computer room swarming with the grey-suited service engineers of a major computer firm, all frantically engaged in attempting to diagnose and correct a major failure of a mainframe computer. By contrast, the senior systems engineer who possessed the expertise necessary to overcome the problem was sitting in the middle of the floor, dressed in jeans and smoking in the no smoking area. No doubt it was only his considerable expertise and acknowledged scarcity value that permitted him to behave in this way!

A more subtle and less visible control operated in all organizations is that of recruitment policy. By being able to select whom it employs, an organization has a very powerful means of influencing employee behaviour. Not only can it select people on the basis of their technical training and ability, but may also take into account a wide range of other factors such as education, attitudes, norms and values. The popularity of interviews as a means of personnel selection, despite their well-documented shortcomings, may be explained by the possibility they allow of a range of unspoken and largely unspecified criteria to be taken into account. Examples range from the merchant bank which selects its staff solely from those who have attended a select number of public schools and universities, to the used car dealer who chooses sales staff on the basis of their appearance and manner. Further, once personnel have been selected, they are often put through programmes of induction and training which may be designed as much to inculcate organizational norms and values as to provide technical expertise.

Once staff have been appointed, a universal feature of all control systems is that subsequent behaviour is controlled by a mixture of rewards and punishments. These rewards may be monetary, but the more powerful controls often do not involve money. For example, the shop floor employee who clocks in late will probably lose pay, but the senior manager who breaks the unwritten rules of appropriate behaviour is more likely to be assigned to some undesirable department or location. On the positive side, those who are seen as conforming to desired practice can be rewarded in a variety of ways. The most obvious is promotion, with its concomitant rewards of status and increased pay, but there may be all manner of other indications of approval.

A particularly wide range of controls can be seen applied to the control of sales reps. Such people are often regarded as difficult to control because they are unaffected by many traditional controls because they work individually and away from company premises. Not surprisingly, they are subject to monetary controls, often being paid a low basic salary supplemented by a percentage commission on sales made. This may be coupled with a further bonus for achieving a sales target or quota set by their sales manager. However, a range of non-monetary rewards is also typically used. Better salespeople may be rewarded with more luxurious versions of the company car, giving them greater status among their peers at relatively little cost to the company. There may be a range of competitive awards, ostentatiously given out at sales conferences. One company sends a catalogue of gifts of household goods to representatives' spouses together with a note of the sales performance required to obtain them; the assumption is evidently that further pressure from the home front will motivate increased effort.

All these mechanisms are designed to encourage salespeople to put in as much effort as possible, directed in the most effective manner. However, most are only feasible because there is a relatively clear measure of performance available: value of sales made. Even in this area the approach can be dysfunctional if salespeople are expected to provide other services to clients, and may encourage them to offer excessive discounts or to overstock clients in order to boost their own measure of performance in a particular time period.

In summary, organizational controls can be specific and quantitative, or more diffuse and qualitative. Only in the former case is the accounting system an important mechanism for control. When desirable behaviour can be precisely defined, or when clear measures of output exist, accounting controls are useful because they can be linked to reward systems that will encourage desirable behaviour. However, in many circumstances and particularly at more senior levels, it is not possible to specify desired behaviour or even desired results in an unambiguous manner, and more qualitative controls become important. In these circumstances accounting controls are still important but it is vital that too much emphasis is not placed on easily measured but imperfect criteria of performance, as it is all too easy to encourage inappropriate behaviour. The art of effective control lies in selecting the correct balance between quantitative and qualitative means of control. The overall aim of the control process is to encourage all employees to direct their best efforts in the interest of the organization. Although technical systems can aid this process, it is fundamentally a matter of influencing human behaviour, and as such requires behavioural and managerial skills in addition to a well-designed accounting information system.

Conclusions

The objective of an accounting control system is to help ensure that organizational activities contribute towards the attainment of overall organizational goals or plans. Ultimately, an effective control system must affect the behaviour of all employees, including those at the lowest levels in the hierarchy. For the system to have an impact on an individual employee, two major conditions must be satisfied. First, the employee must understand precisely what is expected or required of him/her. That is, the control system must communicate goals and plans. Second, the employee must be motivated to try to attain the expectations that have been communicated. In other words, the control system must have appropriate rewards associated with it.

Both these aspects can be assisted by the use of a well-designed accounting control system. For example, a budgetary control system typically breaks down overall organizational plans into objectives for departments and sections. Thus, a given manager will be set precise targets to be attained in a given time period for his/her responsibility centre. Next, by collecting information on actual performance and comparing it with the budget targets, feedback on the effectiveness of task performance can be provided. Coupled with a system of performance appraisal, the use of a budgetary control system can provide strong motivation for individual managers to achieve their budget targets.

Indeed, because accounting and budgetary controls provide such an important means of control, they are ubiquitous in all types of business enterprise. They are such powerful mechanisms that it is important to remind managers that they are incomplete, and need to be supplemented by other controls. This is necessary to ensure that those aspects of performance which cannot be adequately captured by quantitative and financial measures are also monitored and controlled. The next chapter is therefore devoted to considering what the role of budgetary control should be in the overall package of controls that can be used to influence organizational activities.

· 3 ·

The role of budgets
in organizational control

The construction and operation of a set of accountability arrangements and controls that will lead to effective performance is a central part of a manager's task. The most powerful controls are often not based on accounting information at all, but upon direct observation of those most immediately involved or upon personal contact with them. A conversation, a telephone call or a personal visit is usually the most straightforward way of redirecting activities in the desired direction and often provides immediate feedback about the effectiveness of the control actions being implemented. Direct, personal control is the mainstay of all organizational activity. Yet accounting controls, despite their formality and remoteness from day-to-day operations, still have an important role to play.

The importance of accounting information increases as the organizational hierarchy is ascended. At higher levels managers are attempting to control complex operations of great diversity in an environment characterized by change and uncertainty. In such a context the accounting system acts as a vital integrative mechanism which combines the impact of the many varied factors concerned into a measure of organizational effectiveness. Thus a simple accounting statement such as the profit and loss account may be viewed as an overall control measure which summarizes the overall position of the enterprise. Organizational survival depends upon the avoidance of continuing losses, and the accounting system can help pin-point areas of unsatisfactory performance and also aid in the evaluation of alternative courses of action designed to improve matters. Accounting controls thus form a vital part of the control mechanisms available to senior managers.

In addition, effective control requires a standard against which measures of actual performance can be compared. Sometimes this standard is implicit. For example, the minimum level of overall profitability required for sustained survival may not be explicitly calculated but it is likely to be at the back of each senior manager's mind. Certainly the point at which profits turn into losses is so critical as to need no formal standard against which to assess it. But in dealing with parts of the overall enterprise, and in measuring the effectiveness and efficiency of business unit and managerial performance, explicitly formulated standards become essential. This is the function served by the budgetary system, namely the setting of objectives to be attained and the subsequent monitoring of actual results to ensure that activities are running to plan.

There are two main aspects to budgetary control. First, it is a method of planning programmes of activities that are feasible in terms of the many constraints on organizational activity that exist and it acts as a formal mechanism by which conflicts between different interest groups within the organization are resolved. Second, it is a management control device designed to ensure that agreed policies are implemented and to monitor the extent of their achievement against previously established criteria.

Budgetary control is therefore of prime importance in the establishment of effective organizational control although it is not of itself sufficient. It is in no way a substitute for direct managerial observation and action, but rather seeks to monitor activities at a higher level of aggregation. As it is the major formal technique available for overall management control it is of the greatest importance at senior management levels. Such a description of budgeting is not intended to denigrate the importance of less formal methods of control; these are often more important and more effective than any accounting controls. Yet the fact remains that budgeting is often the sole formal integrative control that exists at senior management level. It is admittedly imperfect, but as it may fairly be said that in the kingdom of the blind the one-eyed man is king, so budgeting fulfils a vital role.

Multiple roles of budgeting

The design and operation of systems of budgetary control is inevitably bound up with more encompassing organizational activities. Budgeting is concerned with the setting of objectives and the allocation of scarce resources; it is thus involved in the political processes of conflict resolution within the organization. It is also concerned with monitoring and evaluating the performance of business units and of the managers responsible for them, and it thus strikes to the heart of organizational activity. Budgeting cannot sensibly be viewed solely as a technical accounting activity divorced from its organizational context. It is intimately bound up in much wider and more complex activities and must be studied from this perspective.

The most important feature of any budget system is that it rarely, if ever, is used for just one purpose. Because it is often the only available quantitative measure of organizational performance it is forced into serving multiple purposes and taking on several different roles at different times. Although it is not suggested that any one budget system will necessarily serve all the roles outlined below, it should be borne in mind that most budget systems require several functions to be served by the same accounting numbers.

Authorization

The most straightforward use of a budget is to act as an authorization for a manager to spend a given amount of money on specified activities. This function is most highly emphasized in programme budgets and capital budgets where strict spending limits can be enforced. It is less apparent in operating budgets because over-spending is usually preferable to the cessation of production, but even here strict enforcement of budget limits may be an important managerial tool. The authorization function is closely tied to the formal distribution of responsibility and authority within the organization and with ideas of responsibility accounting. In a decentralized organization budget holders may be given wide discretion as to how they achieve their budgeted profit or cost targets; in a more centralized structure greater attention may be paid as to whether individual budget categories are accurately achieved.

Forecasting and planning

All budgets are based on forecasts, that is, estimates of the likely outcomes of uncontrollable events. For example, forecasts of national and world economic activity, cost and price inflation and consumer preferences are all incorporated into the derivation of profit budgets. These forecasts form the basis for planning, that is, arranging those activities that can be controlled so as best to achieve the organization's purposes. Such planning budgets are important in several ways. First, they are essential for the efficient performance of functional management responsibilities. For example, a financial manager may base the provision of necessary finance upon cash flow estimates derived from budget plans; similiarly a production manager may construct material purchasing schedules from the estimates of required production incorporated into the budget. Second, they may be used by managers in one part of the organization to adapt their activities to fit in with what is happening elsewhere. Both these uses require that planning budgets are based on the best available estimates of the outcomes that are likely to occur.

Planning is an attempt to control the future by current acts. Just like any other control activity it requires a predictive model to forecast the likely outcome of planned activities. Where this predictive model is inaccurate or misleading actions will be taken to avoid eventualities which would in fact not have occurred. Thus planning should be restricted to those areas in which predictions can most confidently be made; where prediction is difficult then planning is pointless and organizational resources might better be devoted to adapting to eventualities as they occur rather than attempting to anticipate them.

Communication and coordination

Budgets can play a part in the communication processes of an organization. They may be used in order to communicate plans to those managers responsible for implementing them although the budget does not usually contain sufficient information to implement a plan. Rather, it is a useful vehicle for conveying quantitative information concerning plans and policy constraints. In addition to communicating information directly relevant to managers in the performance of their jobs, the budget can be helpful in aiding managers in different subunits to coordinate their activities by making them aware of the requirements of others with whom they interact and the constraints they face. The wider dissemination of budgetary information in this way can assist in the development of a supportive organizational climate.

Motivation

Budgets may be used as a means of motivating managers to achieve organizational objectives. However, an external standard only has a motivational effect if it is 'internalized' by the recipients, that is, accepted by them as their own target. Thus it is important to ensure that budgets are accepted by their recipients. One major means of achieving this is to allow managers to participate in setting their own budgets. A great deal has been written about participation in budget setting, but its impact seems to be three-fold. First, participation increases the relevance of the budget standard in the eyes of the recipient; second, it generally improves managers' attitudes to the budget system; and third, it increases the flow of information between managers and their superiors. All of these three effects would seem to be beneficial, but it should not be overlooked that participation also gives managers the opportunity to introduce bias into their estimates if they are motivated to do so.

It has been suggested that budgets only have a positive motivational effect if they represent a challenging target that is achieveable but which carries a risk that it will not be achieved. Budgets designed to motivate may thus not be suitable for planning purposes, which require best estimates. Similarly if budget variances are treated as a sign that someone is at fault, rather than a sign of a healthy system, budgets may soon be met again but cease to have a motivational impact. This subject is discussed at greater length in Chapter 4.

Performance evaluation

The performance of business units and that of the managers in charge of them is often evaluated by reference to budget standards as these form a convenient quantitative reference point. Such evaluation may merely take the form of reporting actual perform- ance against budget and leaving it to the managers themselves to make appropriate use of this feedback information. More usually, however, there will be a more or less formal accountability meeting with a superior at which the manager is required to explain deviations from budgeted performance. The precise way in which performance is evaluated and the consequences that result from this meeting will be a dominating influence on future performance. A strong stress on budget attainment will likely lead to budgets which are more closely met in future, but possibly at the cost of poorer long-term performance and a variety of unfortunate side effects. This theme will be taken up again in Chapter 5.

Of all the roles served by budgetary information it is its role in performance evaluation that is likely to be the most crucial, because it is this role that impacts most strongly upon the middle and junior managers being controlled by the budgetary system. Because rewards (either monetary or non-monetary) are attached to success- ful performance and because success is measured relative to the budgetary standard, there are substantial pressures brought to bear on the budget system. These manifest themselves in three different ways. First, there is a pressure to introduce bias into the budget itself. For example, a manager may attempt to obtain a budget that is relatively easy to attain, as subsequent performance will then be evaluated against a depressed standard. Alternatively an optimistic estimate may be put forward in the hope that anticipation of a successful future will alleviate current criticism. Second, there is a pressure on actual activities. Managers may engage in inappropriate activities, such as failing to maintain plant properly or skimping on quality, in order to stay within budgetary constraints. Third, there is a pressure on reported results. Managers may find that they are able to manipulate the information reported by the accounting system by, for example, switching expenses from one account heading to another, by altering the timing of revenue and expense recognition, or by otherwise creating or exploiting loopholes in the data collection system.

Because the use of budgetary information in performance evalua- tion has such immediate and important effects on the individual manager, it is this use that is likely to have most impact upon the overall budgetary control system. It is necessary to ensure that accounting information is used in appropriate ways in performance evaluation so that the usefulness of the system is not compromised in other areas.

Budgeting as a political process

Because budgeting can serve such a range of diverse purposes the designer of a budgetary control system must balance the different requirements and potential imperfections of competing uses in constructing a system that most nearly matches the needs of the organization. To effectively carry out this task requires an understanding of the fundamental underpinnings of the budgetary process, namely the underlying organizational processes on which budgeting rests.

There are three basic facts of organizational life that condition the operation of a budgetary system. In the first place, resources are scarce and thus require a careful and considered determination of how, when and where they should be used. In most organizations the competing roles of advocates, who present proposals for the use of resources on specific schemes, and guardians, who have to reduce claims to match availabilities, are institutionalized. The role of guardian is often taken by the chief accountant or finance director, for the claims are most readily evaluated in terms of their financial implications. In the second place, each member of the organization has his/her own objectives and priorities, leading to processes of negotiation and bargaining over what should or should not be included in budget estimates. In these processes personal goals and statements of organizational objectives often become conflated and impossible to separate. Finally, the complexity of the operations being managed and the uncertainties inherent in the environment often mean that those who are responsible for integrating an organization's diverse activities into a coherent package are largely ignorant of the detailed nature and value of the underlying activities. This can develop into a tendency towards organizational inertia apparent in an incremental approach to budgeting, where only small changes are made to previously established patterns of activity, and the use of simplistic techniques such as the application of uniform cuts to budgeted expenditures.

These common features of organizational activity result in patterns of budgetary behaviour that recur in all organizations. There are managers concerned with spending pitted against those concerned with gaining revenues and saving; managers more concerned with their own area of operations than that of others; overall viability may seem to be a minor consideration to most participants. The same budgetary practices such as padding, across the board cuts, increased spending towards the end of the budget period and the husbanding of contingency reserves will be observed. Yet there are also substantial differences between budgetary practices in different organizations. Contingency theory (discussed at greater length in Chapter 7) provides a general framework for explaining some of these differences in terms of differences in organizational strategy, environmental uncertainty, task technology and organizational structure, but we still lack specific guidance as to what is the most appropriate system for a particular organization.

Conclusions

The implication for designers of budget systems is clear. They must be responsive to the organizational processes in which budgeting is implicated, for no technical budget features will be able to overcome the powerful organizational forces that are brought to bear on the process of budget formulation and implementation. The budget system is moulded by political processes *not* vice versa. However it is still possible to adapt the budget system so as to work with organizational forces rather than against them. Scarce resources can be better allocated if their value can be accurately assessed; the appropriate action in the face of uncertainty can be better judged if good predictive models of its consequences can be constructed; the effects of complexity can be minimized by better systems for data collection and information processing; and even the complex process of resolving conflicts in values can be aided by the ready availability of relevant factual information. In these and other ways accounting information can contribute to the establishment of effective systems of organizational control.

PART TWO

Application

· 4 ·

Motivating
good performance

One of the most important functions served by accounting information is that of motivating improved performance. The provision of
regular information to give managers feedback on the results of their
activities is an absolute necessity for effective learning. If the
outcomes of actions are not known, or are incorrectly assumed to be
adequate, then performance cannot be monitored and improved.
Knowledge of results is the key to their improvement.

This has been graphically illustrated in the medical field where
the provision of 'bio-feedback' (that is, visible measures of certain
biological functions such as heart rate or sweating) has allowed
patients to develop the ability to control bodily functions previously
thought to be beyond conscious control. Thus, if a standard of what
is desirable is available, feedback concerning the results of actions
allows their efficacy to be assessed and the most effective to be
selected in future. There is an obvious parallel with systems of
budgetary control which define in advance a standard to be attained
and regularly report on the degree to which it is being attained.

However effective self-control requires not only knowledge of
results but also a desire on the part of the individual to progress in
the desired direction. Whereas this is not problematic in a small
owner-managed business it becomes a central issue in larger
enterprises where there may be a complete divorce between
ownership and control. Here managers may be pursuing their own
self-interest which does not automatically coincide with the goals of
the owners (who may be widely dispersed shareholders). To align

managers' actions so that they act in pursuit of organizational goals requires the construction of a system of incentives to reward managers for behaving appropriately. In a large and complex organization the construction of such a performance measurement and reward system is a major task and will be discussed in detail in Chapter 5. For the moment we will concern ourselves solely with the motivational effect of having pre-set targets to be achieved, augmented by reports of actual performance.

What is motivation?

Theories of motivation have abounded since time immemorial. The work of many of the classical writers has been concerned with how to encourage others to do what you wish, perhaps culminating in Machievelli's treatise on maintaining political control. The common thread of such advice has been that there exist certain universal human traits that can be exploited in order to obtain one's way. The role of rewards and punishments is evidently vital, but it is of interest to note that modern writers on management have emphasized less tangible rewards such as the nature of the work itself, the provision of autonomy and responsibility and the cultivation of self-esteem as being of equal importance. But the trend in the development of theories of motivation has been to move away from the identification of specific factors (such as pay systems, working conditions and self-fulfilment) that were believed to be universally associated with high degrees of motivation in most individuals, towards more general formulations that allow for different people to be motivated in different ways.

Such contingent theories recognize that individuals differ in the values that they attach to specific rewards and may well require quite different motivational devices to encourage greater effort. An example of such differences in basic values is implicit in Lord Roben's questioning of a mineworker as to why he turned up for only four shifts each week rather than the expected five; the man's considered response was that he could not live adequately on the wages for three shifts. Here an increase in pay might well have produced less rather than more effort!

Modern motivational theories converge in requiring models to be constructed for specific circumstances rather than aiming for general findings that can be universally applied. Thus we should expect few specific results capable of immediate application but more a framework for thinking about motivational structures that can be used to analyse a specific situation.

The central concept of motivational theory is that of activation. People find different events and activities motivating to different extents. Activation, that is the amount of psychological energy a person has available to deal with a given situation or event is roughly determined by the joint (multiplicative) effect of three factors: the amount of uncertainty about the outcome of an event, its importance and one's ability to influence it. The absence of any one of the three factors will lead to low levels of motivation (Burgoyne, 1975). This model can be represented as:

$$\text{activation} = \begin{array}{c}\text{uncertainty}\\\text{about}\\\text{outcome}\end{array} \times \begin{array}{c}\text{importance}\\\text{of}\\\text{outcome}\end{array} \times \begin{array}{c}\text{ability to}\\\text{influence}\\\text{outcome}\end{array}$$

In a budgetary situation this model suggests that a high degree of activation will occur to the extent that managers are uncertain as to whether they will be able to meet their budget (a challenging target?), the importance they attach to meeting it and the extent to which they believe they are capable of influencing the events that will result in the ultimate outcome.

However, it is important not to confuse activation with motivation. There is a maximum amount of psychological energy that can be constructively utilized. Levels of activation in excess of this maximum will result in destructive consequences and in a condition of 'stress'. Aside from its personal consequences stress also results in less effective performance. This leads to the view that both very low and very high degrees of activation are to be avoided; for a given person and situation there is an optimal level of activation. Deviations from this optimum in either direction will result in a deterioration in performance; overactivation must be guarded against as well as underactivation.

This framework is evidently a much simplified version of real life, but it provides a structure for thinking about motivation. Making a budget target demanding and emphasizing its importance in circumstances where a manager has little control over outcomes can produce stressful levels of activation. When this occurs individuals will invoke various coping mechanisms, such as avoidance and defensive reactions, that are counter-productive. In particular, managers may attempt to discover methods of meeting the budget by engaging in manipulative and dysfunctional activities which once practised are difficult to eradicate.

Finally, it should be noted that motivation is not the only factor involved in obtaining high levels of performance, for good performance requires both motivation and ability (Lawler, 1973). Further, ability itself is a consequence of both innate aptitude and of training and experience. Thus managers seeking to improve their subordinates' performance should be at least as concerned with personnel selection (the matching of aptitudes with task requirements) and education and training as with increasing motivation. Indeed it has been argued (Gilbert, 1978) that direct attempts to increase motivation are one of the *least* powerful methods at a manager's disposal. The greatest effect we can have on people's motives comes through indirect means such as changing the task environment, job redesign and the assignment of greater responsibility.

Thus, although motivation is an important factor in encouraging high levels of attainment, it is equally important to consider the tasks involved and the environment in which they are performed as well as individual psychology. Indeed this is the approach that has been taken by studies of the effectiveness of systems of budgetary control by focusing on target-setting, performance measurement and information feedback, and it is to these topics we now turn.

Budgets as targets

The existence of a budget standard can act as a target to be aimed for. There is substantial evidence from psychological studies that having a defined, quantitative target results in better performance than when no such target is stated (Tosi, 1975). Further, the more difficult and demanding the target set, the better the resulting performance, although targets thought to be unattainable are counter-productive.

Specific targets produce better performance than vague exhortations to 'do your best'. In one study on goal-setting (Meyer, Kay and French, 1965) where performance requirements were translated into specific goals 65 per cent showed subsequent improvement in contrast to only 27 per cent of those which were left non-specific. However, it is important to note that although difficult goals can easily be *assigned* to people they are not necessarily *accepted* by them. If people decide that a goal is impossible to attain they are likely to give up and turn in results that are worse than if a less demanding goal had been set. An industrial study on goal-setting (Stedry and Kay, 1966) found that difficult goals produced either very good or very bad results compared with goals of normal difficulty, with the poor results occurring particularly when several difficult goals were set at the same time. Another study concerned with the evaluation of a system of management by objectives (Carroll and Tosi, 1973) found that difficult goals led to reduced effort on the part of those managers who were less mature and experienced and who had less self-assurance.

The psychological evidence therefore suggests that the best results will be obtained by setting the most difficult goals that will be accepted by managers and thus 'internalized' and accepted as their own personal objectives. A budget has a very strong potential for motivation as it represents a definite, quantitative goal, but the standards it incorporates need to be accepted by those involved before their existence will motivate better performance. The level of difficulty that will be accepted is likely to vary significantly from person to person and may bear little resemblance to the 'tight, yet attainable' accounting adage. Formally agreed budget goals will be more effective than implicit self-set goals only when the formal goals were set at a more demanding level than the self-set goals and when the formal goals are accepted by the manager involved (Locke, 1968).

These findings indicate the importance of participation in budget-setting. Managers who are actively involved in the process of setting their own budget are much more likely to accept the standards incorporated into it. Nevertheless there are also dangers inherent in participative budgeting. Some managers may use the opportunity given by participation to reduce the standards demanded of them and to bias the estimates they submit. Thus participation is no universal panacea; it is an essential part of effective budgetary control, but needs to be used with care and understanding.

Most of the studies referred to above have been experimental.

More reliable evidence on the effects of budget targets in a real organizational context can be obtained from field studies, although only a handful of these exist. One major such study was conducted in a European context by Hofstede (1968). Hofstede was concerned to discover the conditions under which budgets could be used to promote positive attitudes in managing task performance. Previous US-based studies had indicated that although managers saw budgets as being highly relevant, the use of budgets also invoked negative attitudes such as undue pressure, conflict between managers and manipulation of accounting data. European experience, although less well documented, suggested that more positive attitudes to budgets were prevalent but that these existed only because operating managers generally regarded budgets as irrelevant. Hofstede's study therefore set out to try to find the conditions under which budgets could have a high degree of relevance to managers, and thus act as an important motivational device, yet also not have counter-productive side-effects associated with them. His conclusions concerning budget difficulty were:

(a) Budgets have no motivational effect unless they are accepted by the managers involved as their own personal target.

(b) Up to the point where the budget target is no longer accepted, the more demanding the budget target the better the results achieved.

(c) Demanding budgets are also seen as more relevant than less difficult targets, but negative attitudes result if they are seen as *too* difficult.

(d) Acceptance of budgets is facilitated when good upward communication exists. The use of departmental meetings was found helpful in encouraging managers to accept budget targets.

(e) Managers' reactions to budget targets were affected both by their own personality (some managers intensely disliked budgets that they thought they would not achieve) and by more general cultural and organizational norms.

An important implication of these findings is that the budget level which motivates the best performance is one that is somewhat more demanding than the level of performance that will actually be achieved. However, a budget that is likely to be achieved will motivate only a lower level of performance, as shown in Figure 2. The budget level that most usually motivates the optimum results (a challenging target accepted by the manager) is in excess of the average performance actually attained by that manager. But if it is reduced to a less demanding level, actual performance also decreases.

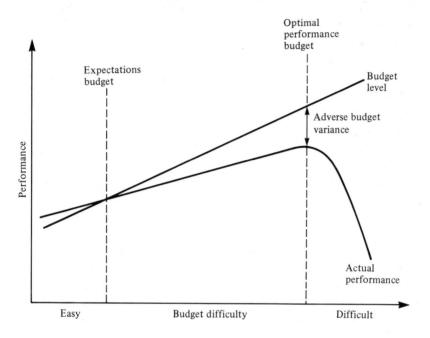

Figure 2 *The effect of budget difficulty on performance*

There is thus a conflict between the planning and control uses of the budget. To motivate the best possible level of actual performance the budget must be set at a level above that which will, on average, be attained. Adverse budget variances will thus be generated, but these are a sign that the budget system is working as intended. A budget that is always achieved with no adverse variances indicates that the standards are too loose to motivate the best possible results. To obtain the desired motivational effects from an appropriately set budget target thus requires that adverse budget variances are treated appropriately; small adverse variances are a healthy sign and should not be treated as something to be avoided.

The attitude of senior managers to adverse budget variances is thus crucial to the successful operation of a truely motivating budget system. If junior managers are strongly criticized whenever their performance is even slightly below budget there is little doubt that less adverse variances will be reported; but the means by which this is achieved will be less than desirable and overall performance is likely to be reduced rather than increased. A further implication of using budgets for motivational purposes is that they become unsuitable for planning purposes. Financial planning requires the best possible estimates of what is likely to occur. Motivational budgets will generally give a more optimistic picture of the future and will require to be amended before being used for planning purposes.

Effects of budgets on performance

There have been a number of more recent studies on the effect various characteristics of budgetary control systems have on managerial performance which have yielded broadly similar conclusions, although it should be noted that they have all been conducted in the USA. One study by Kenis (1979) found that:

(a) Both the clarity of budget-goals and participation in budget-setting were positively associated with job satisfaction, as was the provision of feedback information on budget achievement. Goal clarity and participation were also shown to contribute to higher levels of motivation to meet budgets and with actual budget achievement. In particular, the findings indicate that most managers react well to having budget goals spelt out as clearly and unambiguously as possible.
(b) The idea of a 'tight yet attainable' budget standard appeared to lead to the best actual performance.
(c) Participation in budget-setting tended to improve the degree to which budgets were met but was unrelated to other measures of overall job performance.

This last finding illustrates the problems that exist in assuming that managers who meet their budget are, in fact, performing well. It may solely be that they have obtained a relatively easy budget standard or that they are taking actions that enable them to meet their budgets to the detriment of longer term performance. Other studies, such as those by Ivancevich (1976), Milani (1975) and Steers (1976) have found only relatively insignificant connections between budgetary characteristics and job performance.

A further study by Merchant (1981) has been conducted at an organizational level of analysis. He found that:

(a) Firms which were large, diversified in their activities and decentralized tended to operate a control strategy that could be described as administrative rather than personal in orientation. This involved greater stress on formal control techniques such as budgeting. In these firms lower level managers tended to participate more in budgeting and greater stress was laid on the use, development and achievement of budget targets.

(b) Participation in budget-setting and the emphasis placed on budget achievement by senior managers were both important factors affecting attitudes towards the budget system and the motivation of junior managers to meet the budget.

(c) The contingency theory notion of a 'fit' between organizational characteristics and its environmental context, and the use made of budgets (as indicated in (a) above) was supported in that performance was higher where such a 'fit' was found to exist than where it was not.

In both the two studies outlined participation in budget-setting was found to have significant positive effects on both job satisfaction and performance. However, in a significant extension, Brownell (1981) has found that this link depends upon the personality of the manager involved. Managers who felt that they had a significant degree of control over their destiny exhibited the expected relationship, but those who felt that their destinies were controlled by fate, luck or chance did not. In fact, for such managers increased participation led to lower levels of motivation, satisfaction and performance. Individual differences concerning self-control over one's destiny thus have a marked moderating effect on the consequences of budgetary participation. Participation has a positive motivational effect only upon those managers who are confident in their ability to cope with the many factors that influence job performance; to the extent that they lack such confidence participation only serves to increase their feelings of stress and tension due to uncertainty.

These studies also have implications for the way in which budgetary standards are set. Standards can be derived from basically three sources; past experience of the same operation, what is currently being achieved elsewhere or what is necessary in order to achieve other goals. Standards derived from all three sources can be problematic from a motivational standpoint.

Historical standards based on past experience reflect only what has already been achieved; although suitable for planning purposes they generally require to be modified if they are to act as a motivational target. Standards derived from similar activities being undertaken elsewhere, whether in other parts of the same organization or by competitors, are generally most suited for motivational purposes. The danger in their use is that they may not be perceived as relevant by those to whom they are given. Apparently minor differences in circumstances can cause this type of evidence to be seen as irrelevant by operating managers. Standards based on what is necessary to achieve overall company objectives, although likely to represent challenging targets, suffer from the problem that they may be seen as unrealistic, particularly if the manager to whom they are given was not party to the process of setting those overall objectives.

Nevertheless all three sources of information are valuable in the process of setting budgets that are sufficiently challenging to have a motivational impact yet are accepted by those who work under them as being an attainable target. Such a balance cannot be struck without the active involvement of each individual manager, for some will prefer easier targets yet over-achieve whereas others will accept very difficult goals even if they do not always manage to attain them. Budget-setting can never be reduced to a purely mechanical or technical process; it must be tailored to individual human needs and personalities.

Conclusions

To motivate the best possible level of performance budget standards should represent a challenging target, yet one which the managers concerned believe they may be able to achieve. Such a target cannot be set in any mechanical way but must be tailored to fit the personality of each manager concerned and the characteristics of the operation they are responsible for.

Participation in budget-setting is valuable as it provides an important means of ensuring that budget targets are suited to each of the managers who receive them. Nevertheless its use should be carefully monitored to ensure that it is not used by managers as a means of evading their responsibilities.

Too many difficult goals should not be set at once; rather a budget should provide managers with clear and simple guidance as to what is expected of them.

Frequent and timely feedback on actual results is a necessary condition for improvement.

To encourage innovation managers should be allowed some freedom to fail. If every failure to meet the budget results in immediate criticism, then attempts to discover better ways of performing the job will be discouraged.

Small adverse budget variances are to be expected in a budget system designed to motivate optimum performance. Such variances should be expected and planned for. Senior managers should interpret such variances as a sign that the system is working efficiently and avoid the temptation to criticize their subordinates whenever variances occur.

· 5 ·

Performance
appraisal

Performance appraisal is the foundation stone upon which effective control rests. Managers who know that they will be held to account for their performance will be constantly concerned about the consequences of their current actions. The expectation of future accountability has an immediate and continuing effect: all actions will be evaluated in terms of their impact on future appraisal.

But what is good performance, and how may it be defined in concrete terms? So often the term 'performance' is used to disguise the fact that we cannot specify exactly what is required of a manager. It is certainly unlikely that we shall be able to produce a single objective that the manager should strive to attain, regardless of all other considerations. The achievement of high levels of profit or return on investment may be a very desirable goal, but even such overall goals are subject to numerous constraints, such as the maintenance of liquidity and good relationships with employees. In all practical situations, performance is concerned with achieving a balance between a whole set of goals and constraints.

Once it is admitted that objectives are multiple it also becomes evident that they may conflict with each other, and that trade-offs will inevitably have to be made between that achievement of one objective and another. How much profit should be sacrificed to keep within the overdraft limit? Should product quality be improved in an attempt to increase sales, despite the increased costs involved? Should an industrial dispute be risked in order to introduce more efficient working practices? The list is potentially endless. Every day managers have to make decisions that involve such trade-offs, often with only ambiguous guidance as to what is expected of them.

Performance measures

It has been suggested (Ridgway, 1956) that the multiple nature of practical objectives can lead to an obsessive cycle of behaviour. A single measure of performance is initially emphasized, but it soon becomes evident that it is an inadequate representation of overall good performance. Other measures, representing other important dimensions of performance, are added to it and a battery of performance indicators is thus constructed. However, as these indicators represent partially conflicting objectives, managers soon ask for guidance as to how they should be traded-off against each other. This pressure leads to the construction of a composite measure of performance in which each of the dimensions is weighted into a single overall performance indicator. However, even if the initial weightings give an adequate measure of performance, changing circumstances will ensure that it rapidly becomes obsolete. Other indicators will then be added, and the cycle begins to repeat itself.

Such a process seems quite inevitable as no single measure of performance can ever be adequate to assess the quality of managerial activity. The essence of managerial work is that it involves the exercise of discretion and judgment (Jaques, 1961) and can thus never be precisely specified. Quantitative measurements of results can only give an indication of certain aspects of achievement, for if the work itself demands the exercise of judgment, then the assessment of such work must itself be a matter of judgment.

Once we move from considering the performance of a total business unit and its manager to the performance of subunits, a further range of problems becomes apparent. Interdependence between subunits means that their performance is mutually dependent; to an extent, it is meaningless to talk of the performance of the parts as if they were separate entities. Thus the development of performance measures for parts of an organization involves the following major issues:

1 Organizational purposes are complex and cannot easily be reduced to a single, integrated measure of overall performance.

2   Some tasks are interdependent and require cooperation between subunits; a performance measure for a subunit alone is bound to be inadequate.

3   Some aspects of performance cannot be measured quantitatively.

4   The essence of managerial work is such that the required results cannot be specified in advance; the evaluation of performance must also involve the exercise of judgment.

5   Management takes place in a complex and uncertain environment; it may be inappropriate to reward only achievement alone, as effort may also be deserving of recognition.

Setting standards for performance

The difficulties involved in specifying and rewarding appropriate managerial *behaviour* have led to a concentration on monitoring and rewarding *performance*, despite the above problems. The measures of performance most often used involve accounting information and use budgets as the standard against which results are monitored. Thus, not only are there problems in defining the dimensions of performance to be pursued, but the setting of the level of performance expected on each dimension may also be problematic, particularly in industries subject to rapid environmental change.

The root of the difficulty lies in the imprecision of available predictive models of organizational performance. Not only are we usually ignorant of optimal methods of attaining desired ends, we are sometimes ignorant even of possible methods. Thus, if we do not know how performance is to be achieved, how can we go about laying down standards against which it should be judged?

There are typically five major types of standard against which performance can be compared:

1   The performance of the same unit in previous time periods.
2   The performance of similar units in the same time period.
3   Estimates of expected performance, made in advance.
4   Estimates of what might have been achieved, made after the event.
5   The performance necessary to achieve certain desired goals.

All these standards have inherent defects in the absence of adequate predictive models. Comparison of performance over time periods involves the implicit assumption that all other factors have remained constant; to adjust for the effect of any such differences requires a model of how performance has been affected by such factors. Comparison with similar units assumes that such units exist, information is available, and that each unit faced similar conditions. Standards of potential performance, set in advance require a very complete predictive model; but if such a model exists, there is little problem in appraising subsequent managerial performance! Similarly, setting standards with hindsight is a notoriously difficult exercise to conduct fairly. Finally, comparison with desired goals may not take into account what is actually achievable.

Practical methods of assessing performance usually involve the examination of trends in measures of performance over a period of time. This is a useful pragmatic procedure, but of limited validity in a changing environment; a reduced current performance may still represent an excellent response to changed conditions. Nevertheless, the use of a complete battery of trends, involving all five standards of comparison, can provide a means of making an informed judgment about the overall performance of a unit. The provision of such information, with appropriate comparisons highlighted, is a useful exercise that can be undertaken by a management accountant, and can provide the database from which detailed negotiations on the setting of budget standards can proceed.

If the rewards attached to good performance are such that they will motivate managers to work hard to attain them, it is also likely that the budget standard will come under considerable pressure. Further, the accounting information itself may be manipulated to give the impression of improved performance where this, in fact, has not been achieved. Finally, and most seriously, actual behaviour may be affected so that desired results may be reported, despite the fact that these may have been achieved in undesirable ways. The problem of bias in budget estimates and the manipulation of reports of actual performance is sufficiently important to require a section of its own.

Bias in budget estimates

Although the technical process of constructing budgets is straight-forward, if necessarily complex, the critical problems arise out of the use that is made of the budget system in performance evaluation. The major area of potential conflict arises when budgetary information is used as a forecast of future events, when budgetary standards are used as motivational targets, and when actual results are compared with budgetary standards as a means of evaluating managerial and unit performance. We shall consider the impact of such budgetary bias and manipulation of accounting information on the process of performance appraisal.

If a manager's performance will be evaluated against a previously established budget, then it is evidently in the manager's own interest to ensure that the budget standard is set at an easier rather than a more difficult level of attainment; that is, the manager may be motivated to incorporate 'slack' into the budget estimates (Schiff and Lewin, 1970). There is evidence that such slack is more likely to be built up in good years and converted into reported profits in poor years (Williamson, 1964). Somewhat paradoxically there is also evidence that managers facing very tough environmental conditions will bias budget estimates in the opposite direction and set themselves budgets that are unlikely to be achieved (Otley, 1978); in these circumstances the gains from promising good performance outweigh the consequences of subsequently not attaining it, perhaps illustrating sequential attention to those goals currently felt to be dominant. However, it should be recognized that many managers are principally concerned to use budgets to help them do as good a job as possible, and that budget bias may be a less significant problem in practice than is sometimes suggested.

The most complete analysis of the incorporation of bias into budget estimates is given in a study of the sales budgeting process of a chain of retail shops (Lowe and Shaw, 1968). Three major causes of budget bias were put forward:

1 The reward system of the company which placed a strong emphasis on rewarding performance measured relative to the budget. Good performance, in comparison with the budget, attracted salary increments, bonuses and possible promotion.

2   The influence of past company history, which had involved an implicit belief that sales would continue to grow as they had done in the past. Managers therefore felt under pressure to budget for a continuing increase even where they felt this was unlikely.
3   The insecurity of some managers who, because of their recent poor performance, felt obliged to promise better performance in the future and incorporated optimistic estimates into their budgets.

All three causes of bias involved rational economic behaviour on the part of the managers concerned. In the first case, slack would be incorporated into the budget so that it would be easier to attain in the future. In the second and third cases, optimistic budgets would be submitted in the hope that these would gain current approval, even at the risk of future disappointment.

Such bias in budget estimates may be part of a more general tendency of managers to distort the information they pass to their superiors, so that unfavourable items are underemphasized. This may be a deliberate policy on the part of an ambitious manager who hopes to be promoted before the true situation emerges; or it may be unintentional, as when a manager fails to get round to mentioning problems before a meeting is terminated unexpectedly.

Evidently the opportunity for such bias is constrained by the ability of senior managers to make their own predictions of what should occur, although this ability is often dependent upon information supplied by the subordinate. The problem lies both in the detection and correction of inaccuracies. Detection is difficult because observed errors may be in either direction and caused by changes in external circumstances, or by inadequate forecasting models as well as by deliberate intention. Even if bias is detected, it may not be thought wise to alter budget estimates beause of the potential adverse motivational effect on the subordinate, although private adjustments can be made. Indeed, it seems likely that 'black books' (i.e. private budget estimates) are as an important part of budgetary procedures in many organizations as are the formal systems.

It is also necessary to distinguish between the performance of a business unit and the performance of the manager in charge of it. Summary measures of performance do not indicate the external and internal circumstances against which managers have to battle in order to achieve their results. The best managers may report the worst results because they have been deliberately assigned to the operating unit having the most problems, in an attempt to resolve them and turn the unit around.

There have been a number of attempts to produce accounting reports that try to distinguish between managerial and unit performance, with managers being held responsible only for those factors deemed to be within their control (Solomons, 1965; Amey and Egginton, 1973). However, although these reports isolate one important factor (i.e. degree of control), they do not make any attempt to assess the impact of other features of the external and internal environment which may affect performance. Further, it may be argued that it is part of the manager's job to anticipate and react to the so-called uncontrollable factors. For even if certain factors cannot be controlled, it is possible they can be predicted and steps taken to guard against the adverse consequences. Finally, even where the factors could not be predicted, perhaps it would be regarded as part of the manager's duty to prepare his/her unit so that it could respond flexibly to whatever situation developed.

Thus, traditional ideas of responsibility accounting have only a limited applicability. There is undoubtedly an element of wisdom in ensuring that managers are not held responsible for the poor performance of one of their colleagues, but there are also circumstances where no clear dividing line can be constructed and the attempt to specify a precise division of responsibilities may be counter-productive. In addition, the vagaries of the external environment may be better viewed as an enemy that requires to be outsmarted rather than as an uncontrollable factor that is outside the manager's competence to affect.

Where accurate budget estimates are necessary (e.g. for corporate financial planning) it may well be that better accuracy is obtained by using forecasting models unconnected with the normal budget process; indeed many corporate financial planning models seem to be constructed and used in this way. But despite the imperfections in constructing budget standards, accounting measurement procedures are used and recognized to be valuable in a wide variety of organizations. Managers seem to use the imperfect accounting measures in more complex ways than is commonly suggested in accounting texts, and we now turn to consider some different managerial styles of using accounting information in performance appraisal.

Using accounting information in performance appraisal

The most direct impact of accounting information on managerial behaviour occurs when it is used as a basis for performance evaluation. That is, if managers believe that their performance will be evaluated on the basis of accounting numbers, then they will be concerned to influence those numbers so as to present themselves in the most favourable light. Although this may be in the best interests of the organization, it may also induce a whole range of harmful side effects, many of which have been documented in the accounting literature. Both the way in which accounting information is used by senior managers and the personalities of their subordinates have been shown to have an important effect.

Concern with how accounting information is used has been evident for a considerable period. The use of accounting information in performance appraisal often created behaviour that is not expected, and the magnitude of the unintended negative consequences can be alarming. Most of the early studies of accounting information system use (e.g. Argyris, 1952) suggested that if certain human relations aspects could be sorted out then the accounting and information systems would work as they were designed to. Interestingly, the focus of much early research, and indeed much current research, has been on the operation of budgetary control systems, as these have been recognized as having a pervasive influence in a wide range of organizations.

When budgets are used as standards against which performance is subsequently evaluated, rewards become directly connected with budget achievement. Managers wishing to obtain a good evaluation will clearly be motivated to achieve their budget targets. The problems of designing and operating an effective system of budgetary control largely devolve into the construction of a set of performance measures which, if achieved, will result in the desired overall performance of the organization. There is usually little difficulty in motivating managers to aim to achieve the specified results; what is difficult is ensuring that they are achieved in the intended manner, rather than in ways detrimental to the organization.

The difficulties in specifying and rewarding appropriate managerial behaviour have led to a concentration on the monitoring and rewarding of results (i.e. output controls). The most commonly used measures of performance involve accounting measures of results and use budgets as the standard against which performance is assessed. If the rewards are such as to motivate managers to attain them, it is likely that the budget standard itself will come under considerable pressure, and also that accounting data concerning actual performance will be biased or manipulated to give the impression of good performance where, in fact, this does not exist. Finally, and most seriously, actual behaviour may be modified so that desired results appear to be obtained, although they may be brought about in an undesirable manner.

Despite these problems, accounting measurement procedures are used and recognized to be of value in a wide variety of organizations. Some of the problems associated with the use of accounting performance measures appear to be avoided by managers using the imperfect accounting information in more complex ways than is suggested in the technical accounting literature.

Style of accounting information use

One important study is that conducted by Hopwood (1972), who distinguished between a rigid (budget-constrained) use of accounting information and a more flexible (profit-conscious) style. This study indicated that where accounting information was an imperfect means of measuring actual performance, the use of a rigid evaluative style was inappropriate and led to high degrees of job related tension, poor relationships with both colleagues and subordinates, and a variety of other dysfunctional consequences, such as the manipulation of accounting data. However, the more flexible style avoided many of these harmful side effects while still emphasizing the importance of firm cost control.

Thus, in the situation studied by Hopwood, which observed operating units having a high degree of mutual interdependence, the more flexible style of budget use was considered to be the most effective, although it should be noted that many of the managers

observed made no use at all of accounting information for performance evaluation. Unfortunately Hopwood did not go on to study the
methods these managers used to control their subordinates. It was
also noted that a subordinate manager's choice of style was affected
by that adopted by his/her superior and that a contagion effect was
identified whereby the rigid style could be transmitted downwards
through the organization despite the problems it engendered.

A subsequent study by Otley (1978) deliberately chose to observe
a situation where budgetary and accounting information represented a more adequate basis for performance evaluation. By
selecting an organization consisting of independent profit centres
he found that the rigid style of performance evaluation did not lead
to an increase in the type of harmful consequences observed by
Hopwood, although quite wide variations in style of budget use and
budgetary manipulation were observed. However, these were
largely explained by variations in the circumstances of the units
being managed. It appeared that successful units operating in a
favourable environment tended to be evaluated quite rigidly against
their budget targets, which were generally set quite accurately. By
contrast, less successful units operating in less favourable conditions
were evaluated more flexibly, and their budget targets tended to be
set at optimistic levels and thus achieved only rarely. These results
seem to indicate that managerial style of budget use is not an
independent variable, selected at the choice of a senior manager, but
may be significantly influenced by external circumstances.

Comparison of the two studies also indicates another important
situational difference. Hopwood's study was based on cost centres
having a high degree of interdependence, whereas Otley's was based
on profit centres that were largely independent of each other.
Because budgetary measures of performance become less appropriate as the degree of interdependence increases, managers necessarily
had to use the accounting information in a more flexible manner if
they were to remain effective.

The impact of uncertainty

More recently, Hirst (1981) has sought to place these results in a
wider context by noting that accounting standards of performance
will be a less complete description of adequate job performance in

conditions of high uncertainty. He argues that a medium to high reliance on accounting performance measures will minimize the incidence of dysfunctional behaviour in situations of low task uncertainty, whereas only a medium to low reliance on accounting data is appropriate in conditions of high uncertainty. A later study by Govindarajan (1984) also suggests that managers are likely to evaluated in a more subjective manner if their unit faces a high degree of uncertainty. It is significant that the observed style of performance evaluation adopted was regarded as resulting from environmental conditions rather than from individual personality traits. This study clearly supports Hirst's conclusion that high reliance on accounting measures of performance under conditions of uncertainty is likely to prejudice effective performance.

The central finding of these studies relevant to the impact of accounting control is two-fold. First, it is the way in which accounting information is used by managers and the rewards that are made contingent upon budget attainment that are critical in determining the impact of the control system. Second, the effect of high reliance on budgetary measures of performance is contingent upon circumstances such as the degree of knowledge we have about how managerial behaviour contributes towards successful performance (often low) and also the uncertainty that exists in the external environment of the organization. When faced with internal and external uncertainty of this sort, what may be required is a reward system that is supportive of innovation and which avoids penalizing occasional failure, for only then will managers feel able to devote their efforts towards achieving success rather than avoiding failure.

Individual personality

In addition to the situational factors discussed above, it has also been suggested that a variety of individual personality factors affect how managers use accounting information. In particular, cognitive style and locus of control have been used to explain differences in the way information is perceived and processed.

Cognitive style is that aspect of personality that is concerned with the way in which a person structures and processes information obtained from a wider environment (Doctor and Hamilton, 1973). One conceptual scheme differentiates people as being either field-dependent (low analytic) or field-independent (high analytic) according to their ability to pick out information from its context. Thus a high analytic person will approach a problem by selecting information from its context on the basis of some conceptual model of the situation; a low analytic person will tend to see the situation more holistically and be more influenced by the context in which the information is embedded. Benbaset and Dexter (1979) conducted an experiment using a business simulation that indicated cognitive style influenced profit performance, decision time and accounting report request behaviour. It appeared that structured-aggregated accounting information (e.g. income statements, balance sheets, cost reports and funds flow statements) were well suited to high analytic types; after all, such statements are essentially models which allow a complicated situation to be structured. By contrast, this type of information appeared to act as a hindrance to low-analytic types who performed better when provided with disaggregated raw data.

This study provides some evidence to suggest that aspects of personality such as cognitive style can be important factors in determining the appropriate type of accounting information to provide to managers. Indeed, it has been suggested that accounting system designers should provide information to decision makers in a format that is compatible with their cognitive style (Macintosh, 1985). However, other results have been less clear-cut. For example, Otley and Dias (1982) found that cognitive style had no discernible effect on information use, although such null results may be a consequence of the fact that most managers tend to be high analytic types, and that the sample selected did not show sufficient variation.

Another personality variable that has been studied is locus of control, or the degree to which people accept personal responsibility for what happens to them. People with an external locus of control tend to see events as being unrelated to their own behaviour and thus beyond their personal control; those with an internal locus believe that they have a substantial influence over their destiny. An experiment conducted by Brownell (1981) investigated the interaction of locus of control with participation in budget-setting. This confirmed the expected interaction; those with an internal locus of control performed best and learnt most quickly when allowed to participate in budget-setting. By contrast, those with an external locus did best when targets were set for them, without participation. These results suggest that people who find themselves working under conditions which complement their personality learn faster, and consequently perform better, than when there is a mismatch.

Conclusions

It can therefore be deduced that the appropriate design of a system of performance evaluation, and the appropriate use of accounting information within such a system, is affected both by external, contingent factors and by individual personality characteristics. The accounting information system needs not only to be tailored to the circumstances of the organization, but quite possibly also to the characteristics of the people working within it. Modern computer-based information systems have the potential to allow such a system to be established, although there is no evidence that it has been attempted in practice.

All this implies that, although accounting information has an important role to play in performance evaluation, it has to be used in a way that takes account of its limitations. As any accounting system is an imperfect tool, it is the way in which senior managers make use of the information it provides which will determine the response of their subordinates. Further, it is possible that the lack of use of accounting information is as serious a problem as its misuse, particularly at middle manager level (Dew and Gee, 1973). Line managers will ignore formally produced accounting information when they perceive it to have little relevance to their needs, and may develop alternative sources of information that are of more value to them, as Mintzberg (1975) indicates in his outline of the impediments to the use of management information. Here the responsibility lies with the accounting information systems designer to develop a deeper understanding of the information requirements of specific tasks so as to be able to provide more relevant information.

It is not possible to spell out specific recommendations for the accounting information systems designer, but the following issues require resolution in every implementation:

(a) What dimensions of performance should be the subject of quantitative measures, and which should be considered only in qualitative terms?

(b)   To what extent should trade-offs between the various performance measures used be explicitly specified?

(c)   To what extent should managers be allowed to participate in
setting the standards against which their performance will be
evaluated?

(d)   What other trends and benchmarks should be used in
evaluating actual performance?

(e)   How will budgetary bias be detected, monitored and controlled?

(f)   How will managerial performance be distinguished from unit
performance?

(g)   How rigidly or flexibly should accounting information be used
in performance evaluation?

(h)   In what ways will uncertainty and individual personality
differences be taken into account in operating the budgetary
control system?

· 6 ·

The aggregation of accounting information

In Chapter 4 and 5 we have been primarily concerned with the setting of budget standards for subordinates and the subsequent appraisal of their performance by their immediate superior. However, in a large organization, accounting information passes through a number of hierarchical levels, and the progress of information through the organization raises a number of new issues.

We first need to consider the reasons why accounting information is an important source of information for senior managers, particularly in diversified organizations. The basic reason is quite straightforward: accounting provides the only common language in which the details of the operations of a wide range of operating subsidiaries can be summarized. Whereas in an organization manufacturing a single product it is meaningful to discuss the total output of the organization in physical terms (e.g. tonnes of coal, barrels of oil, etc.), this is not possible where multiple products are concerned. At the other extreme, in a multidivisional organization having operating subsidiaries in different industries (e.g. farming, electronics, metalworking, papermaking and animal products, to name a few of the activities of one UK company) there is no way in which information about all the operations can be aggregated, except in monetary terms. Thus accounting information such as sales revenues, production costs, profit margins and return on investment provides the common language which can be used to compare and contrast the results obtained by each activity.

There are further reasons for the extensive use of accounting information at senior levels in companies. Profit and return on investment are goals which the total organization is aiming to achieve; adequate control requires constant feedback on actual performance in these terms. Financial information is also important for central financial management, such as the maintenance of liquidity and an appropriate financial structure. But senior general managers use accounting information for control purposes primarily because there are few other sources of quantitative information that can be validly used to assess the performance of diverse operating subsidiaries. Although this use of accounting information is of most importance in diversified, multidivisional organizations, where there is usually little alternative information, accounting information is still of considerable importance at senior levels in all organizations.

Not only are senior managers reliant on accounting reports of actual performance for vital control information, they also require budgetary data to act as a standard against which the actual results can be compared. Although figures of profit and return on investment can be compared against some intuitive standards (e.g. profit v loss; return on investment v desired overall return on investment), these provide only crude standards of comparison which do not take into account differences in internal and external circumstances. Similarly, although trends over time can provide useful insight into patterns of improvement or deterioration, they do not explicitly attempt to predict what could have been expected. Thus the budget standard is important because it represents a previously set standard of performance which has incorporated the opinions of those most closely connected with the situation.

Participation in budget-setting by managers who will subsequently be evaluated by reference to the budget is a vital part of the control process, even though it may make the figures less suitable for planning purposes. Again, because budget standards will have been used to produce aggregate estimates of corporate performance, comparison of actual results with the budget is still an important exercise, even when circumstances have changed between the time when the budget is set and when results are reported, although standards of what might have been achieved had the new situation been predicted, are also useful.

However the use of budgets in this way is not without its problems. To act as a valid standard of comparison, it is necessary that the budget is set at similar levels of difficulty for all managers in all operating subsidiaries. But this is unlikely to occur. Different managers are likely to be most effectively motivated by targets set at different levels of difficulty. Some will respond best to challenging targets, whereas others would feel threatened by such targets and work best with more conservative estimates. Further, although the use of budgets as motivational targets may be their most important feature at junior and middle levels of management, senior managers require budget estimates that represent accurate forecasts of expected outcomes for planning purposes. Where budgets are set primarily to motivate operating managers to achieve optimum performance, they will represent targets that are not, on average, expected to be achieved. It is therefore necessary to analyse what occurs when such optimistic estimates are aggregated up the hierarchial levels of an organization. This will lead us on into the more general problems of using single point estimates of uncertain outcomes, and wider issues in the management of uncertainty. Finally, the construction of performance reports for interdependent subsidiaries raises further relevant issues.

Aggregation of budget estimates

We take as our starting point the observation that budgets are often set at levels that do not represent expected levels of performance. On the one hand, the budget may represent an optimistic assessment of performance, set for motivational reasons or because of the incorporation of bias by junior managers keen to gain current approval. On the other hand, the budget may represent a conservative assessment of likely performance because the manager does not wish to raise expectations of what actual performance may be before it occurs. Our concern in this section is to explore the implications of aggregating budgets that have likelihoods of achievement that differ from expected values.

Consider first the very simple case where a number of subordinate managers are in charge of operating units having identical characteristics and producing a single product. All the managers report to a single superior and we will assume that they all submit output budgets having the same chance of being achieved. In the numerical example given we shall also assume that output follows a normal distribution for ease of calculation, although this is not necessary for the general argument (Otley and Berry, 1979). Although this example describes only a highly idealized situation, it serves to illustrate some of the most important characteristics of the budget aggregation process.

Let us suppose that output per period is distributed such that it has an expected value of 5000 tonnes and a standard deviation of 1000 tonnes for each plant. It follows (from tables of the normal distribution) that a manager who submits a budget of 5520 tonnes can expect to achieve (or over-achieve) it about 30 per-cent of the time, as 5520 tonnes represents a level of $((5520-5000)/1000=)$ 0.52 standard deviations above the mean. Table 1 shows the result of nine such managers behaving in this manner. In aggregate, they will submit a budget totalling 49,680 tonnes (i.e. 9×5520).

Table 1 *Aggregation of nine identical budget estimates*

Unit	Expected output	Standard deviation	Original submission	Revised submission	Probability of attainment
A	5000	1000	5520	5173	43%
B	5000	1000	5520	5173	43%
C	5000	1000	5520	5173	43%
D	5000	1000	5520	5173	43%
E	5000	1000	5520	5173	43%
F	5000	1000	5520	5173	43%
G	5000	1000	5520	5173	43%
H	5000	1000	5520	5173	43%
I	5000	1000	5520	5173	43%
Aggregate	45,000	3000	49,680	46,560	30%

Each of the nine identical operating units submits a budget having a 30 per cent chance of attainment. The aggregate budget now has only a 6 per cent chance of being attained, as it is set at a level equivalent to 1.56 standard deviations from the aggregate mean. If the total is now revised so that it has a 30 per cent chance of being attained, and the original submissions are adjusted *pro rata*, then the revised individual budgets now each have a 43 per cent probability of being attained.

In order to calculate the chance of the aggregate budget being achieved, it is necessary to note that the distribution of aggregate output is also normal in shape, with an expected value of 45,000 tonnes (i.e. 9 × 5000 tonnes) and a standard deviation of 3000 tonnes (i.e. ($\sqrt{9}$ × 1000), on the assumption that the unit outputs are independent of each other. The aggregate budget of 49,680 tonnes therefore lies some 4680 tonnes above the mean, equivalent to 1.56 standard deviations, and thus having a probability of achievement of just 6 per cent.

The effect of aggregation is quite startling. Each of the nine managers submit budgets having a quite reasonable 30 per cent chance of attainment. When added together, this results in an aggregate budget having a mere 6 per cent chance of being achieved. A challenging motivational budget aggregates into an impossible overall target. To maintain the aggregate probability of achievement at 30 per cent requires that the individual budgets are each reduced to 5173 tonnes, which now have a 43 per cent chance of being achieved. The loss of credibility that can occur when mildly optimistic budgets are aggregated is a potentially serious problem.

This simple example can be extended by considering operating units of different sizes. Such an example is given in Table 2 where units having expected outputs ranging from 1000 tons to 9000 tonnes are aggregated. It should be noted that the standard deviations of the units' output have been adjusted in proportion to the square root of expected output, this being the most realistic assumption that can be made (see Otley and Berry, 1979 for a justification). It can be seen that the aggregation process produces similar results to before: budget estimates having a 30 per cent chance of attainment aggregate into a total budget having only a 7 per cent chance of attainment.

However, if a pro rata adjustment is made to preserve the 30 per cent chance of attainment of the aggregate budget, not only does the probability of attaining the unit budgets change, it changes differently for different units! In particular, the smallest unit now has a revised budget that has a 36 per cent chance of attainment whereas the largest unit has a revised budget that is likely to be attained 46 per cent of the time. Thus the apparently uncontroversial feature of pro rata budget revison leads to individual budgets having widely different probabilities of attainment despite their being submitted with identical probabilities.

Table 2 *Aggregation of budget estimates for units of different size*

Unit	Expected output	Standard deviation	Original submission	Revised submission	Probability of attainment
A	1000	450	1234	1161	36%
B	2000	630	2328	2190	38%
C	3000	775	3403	3202	39%
D	4000	895	4465	4201	41%
E	5000	1000	5520	5193	42%
F	6000	1095	6569	6180	43%
G	7000	1185	7616	7165	44%
H	8000	1265	8658	8145	45%
I	9000	1340	9697	9123	46%
Aggregate	45,000	3000	49,490	46,560	30%

Each original submission has a 30 per cent chance of attainment, giving the total of these submissions only a 7 per cent chance of attainment. If the total is adjusted so that it now has a 30 per cent chance of attainment, and a *pro rata* adjustment is made to each of the original submissions, their revised probability of being attained is shown in the table.

Our conclusion is therefore that the techniques of budgetary aggregation adopted by an organization need to be constructed with the above issues in mind. Rather than imposing arbitrary rules of thumb, such as pro rata adjustment, which distort the underlying figures, the aggregation process should be adjusted to meet the needs of the budgetary process. In particular, if it is accepted that budget estimates may legitimately be set at levels that represent other than expected outcomes, perhaps for motivational reasons, then more sophisticated means of aggregation than simple addition are required. In some cases it may be that arithmetical tidiness should be sacrificed in order to preserve other features of the budget such as constant probabilities of achievement. If so, we may need to learn to live with budgets that do not add up!

We have therefore noted the following effects:

(a) Budget estimates which are initially submitted as mildly optimistic forecasts become grossly optimistic when aggregated.

Conversely, estimates which are initially pessimistic become grossly pessimistic.

(b) The effect will become more pronounced the greater the degree of initial optimism, the greater the number of units being aggregated, and the greater their mutual independence.

(c) Quite small degrees of initial optimism give rise to quite unacceptable degrees of optimism in aggregate budgets.

(d) Pro rata adjustment of individual budget estimates to ensure that an acceptable total figure is maintained can lead to unfair discrimination between operating units of different sizes.

(e) If budget estimates that represent a constant probability of attainment at each hierarchical level are required, then arithmetical additivity has to be sacrificed. The total budget for the organization can legitimately be less than the sum of the individual operating budgets.

The management of uncertainty

The problem of aggregation that is discussed above is a consequence of attempting to make a precise forecast of results in an uncertain world. A typical budget, by its very nature, represents a single point estimate of what may occur in the future. Yet we realize when we make such an estimate that it represents only one possible outcome, and that many other outcomes may occur. There are two possible ways forward, although both have inherent problems. The first is only to use budget estimates that represent the most likely performance to be achieved; the second is to use some form of probabilistic forecast, such as estimating a range of possible outcomes that is expected to include the result that will actually occur.

The most common solution is to use a point estimate representing most likely performance. However, this immediately allows the role of the budget as a financial planning tool for senior management to dominate its motivational role for their subordinates, unless a dual budget system is operated. Such a dual system would involve having one set of estimates for subordinates and a second, different, set for senior management. Such a scheme has been suggested in the past (Stedry, 1960) but it does not seem to have been significantly adopted in practice. However, it may be that companies who operate such a scheme quite understandably do not publicize the fact!

The process of having a factor that is deducted at successive stages in the process of the budget up the organizational hierarchy is observed in practice, although it is often regarded as an undesirable quirk that should be eliminated. The above analysis indicates the legitimate reasons for operating such a scheme, and it may also be true that managers' own 'black book' estimates serve a similar function.

However, even if all budgets were set on the basis of most likely performance estimates, the problem of aggregation may still remain. This can occur if the underlying probability distributions of output, cost and revenue are not symmetric but skewed. There is consider-able reason to expect probability distributions of output and revenue to be negatively skewed, and for distributions of cost to be positively skewed (Otley, 1985). If this is indeed so, then the most likely outcome does not coincide with the mean of the skew distribution. The most likely actual revenue will be greater than the average expected revenue, and the most likely actual cost will be less than the average expected cost. Thus if most likely estimates are used, average actual outcomes will be worse than those budgeted, and the budget will appear to have been optimistically biased in retrospect. The estimates will also suffer from the aggregation problem des-cribed in the previous section.

A possible way around the problem is to use expected (average) values rather than most likely values as budget estimates, but such numbers do not necessarily represent a pattern of performance that is at all realistic, and they may therefore not be suitable for motivational and control purposes. An alternative approach is to abandon single point estimates and move towards incorporating probabilistic forecasts into budgets. The simplest way of doing this would be to estimate cost and revenue ranges, such that actual performance has a predefined probability of actually falling within the defined range. However, although probabilistic forecasts have been built into financial planning models, in practice they do not appear to be popular for control purposes.

Attempting to assess the performance of managers operating in an uncertain environment is a difficult task, particularly when no independent model of expected performance is available. Consider a company that wishes to invest in ten risky projects, each having a 90 per cent chance of success, but a 10 per cent chance of failure. Thus nine projects are expected to be successful and to compensate for the one that is expected to fail. However, suppose the company assigns one manager to each project. At the end of the period it will evaluate their respective performance. The manager in charge of the unsuccessful project may well argue that the outcome is not a reflection of his/her poor performance, but was anticipated at the outset. Even if this is absolutely true, it would still be unlikely that the manager will receive as much praise or enhance his/her promotion prospects as much as his/her colleagues who were fortunate enough to have successful outcomes.

What is likely to happen in practice is that all the managers concerned will adapt their projects to make them less risky, even at the cost of reducing the expected returns. The company is thus likely to end up with ten modestly successful projects yielding less than the nine more successful outcomes planned, although each of the managers concerned may feel happier with the amended situation.

There is no simple answer to such a problem, and it is certainly not one that can be solved purely by the provision of better accounting information. However, as all business situations are inherently risky, to a greater or lesser extent, the appropriate use of accounting information to assist in monitoring, controlling and evaluating managerial performance is an important, if unresolved, issue. All that can be done here is to alert the reader to the problem, and to suggest that the budgetary procedures observed in practice that do not conform to textbook models may, in fact, represent attempts to cope with the underlying uncertainty of the real world. At present we know far too little about the problem to be able to give simple prescriptions.

Problems of interdependence

We have so far considered the problems of using accounting information for control purposes when the operating units concerned are independent of each other. However this is somewhat of an extreme case; in most instances operating units have some degree of interdependence. Although this reduces some problems, such as the aggregation of non-mean estimates, it creates a number of others which will be discussed now.

Interdependence can take several forms. A decision to invest in a specific project constrains expenditure on other projects; there is interdependence between the short and the longterm; and there is interdependence of work flows, products and services with which we will be primarily concerned. Thompson's (1967) categorization of pooled, sequential and reciprocal interdependence is particularly useful.

Pooled interdependence is characterized by operating units that do not interact directly, but who share a common source for a scarce resource (e.g. central provision of capital or of computer facilities). Sequential interdependence occurs when the output of one unit becomes the input of another (e.g. in an integrated steel works), and reciprocal interdependence occurs when the outputs of several units become the inputs for others (e.g. a chemical plant or a manufacturing job shop). As we move from pooled to sequential to reciprocal interdependence, the complexity and the degree of interdependence increases substantially, and a high degree of adaptive coordination is necessary (Thompson, 1967). Traditional accounting mechanisms of control become inadequate and need to be supplemented by other, more adaptive, controls.

Indeed, it has been argued by Baumler (1971) that conventional accounting control based on profit performance targets is clearly not an adaptive process based on mutual agreement; rather it contributes to the illusion of separation between subunits. The results of his laboratory experiment testify to the inappropriateness of using specific targets under conditions of extensive interdependence. Such targets resulted in improved performance only when interdependence was minimal; otherwise they reduced it. Other styles of using accounting information are necessary when a high degree of interdependence occurs, perhaps following Hopwood's profit-conscious and non-accounting styles (Hirst, 1981).

However, despite the problems in interpreting and using such accounting information, it is still produced. Interdependence between operating units can be handled in accounting terms, either by cost allocation or by transfer pricing. A spectrum of alternative treatments can be observed in practice ranging from non-allocation, through various forms of cost apportionment and negotiation, to systems based on charges for actual usage. These latter systems may be based on transfer prices, defined as a monetary value placed on the transfer of goods and services from one unit to another in the same company. In theory and practice, transfer prices can be attached to the movement of goods or services under all three forms of interdependence, and the cost allocation methods of apportionment, negotiation or actual usage each have counterparts in transfer pricing.

Both cost allocation and transfer pricing represent mechanisms which allow accounting statements to be drawn up for operating units *as if they were* independent profit centres. In some cases this may not cause too great a degree of distortion. Where the bulk of an operating unit's trade is external to the company, and where internally provided goods and services are provided at market rates (or a close approximation thereto), no particular problems arise. However where a substantial proportion of trade is conducted internally, and where reliable market prices do not exist, the accounting statements that can be produced lose their significance. But they do so in an insidious manner that cannot be detected from the accounting report.

Essentially, the operating unit moves from being a true profit centre to being a pseudo-profit centre. The form of the accounting statement is unchanged, but its meaning is dramatically altered. From being a fair representation of the performance of the unit as an independent entity, it becomes an accounting fiction that includes large sums allocated or transferred on an essentially arbitary basis (Thomas, 1971). Such a change in meaning is particularly dangerous because the *form* of the accounting statement does not change: the pseudo-profit centre appears to be identical to a normal profit centre. But the meaning of the figures has altered drastically, and they may contain little of economic substance.

There is a great pressure to create profit centres for accounting control, because a true profit centre can be controlled in a very straightforward manner. Provided a balance between costs and revenues is maintained such that adequate profits are being earned, little attention needs to be paid to the details of internal operation. These can be left to the manager of the operating unit, and his/her performance evaluated against budgeted profit targets. But this ease of control generates a pressure to categorize as many units as possible as profit centres, even when this requires the allocation of large items of cost and the extensive use of transfer prices unrelated to market prices. Here the profit centre is transformed into a pseudo-profit centre and the apparent exercise of control becomes an illusion.

One has only to consider the car firm whose production and assembly units were apparently profitable, but whose marketing division made a substantial loss to realize the dangers involved. There was a great temptation to conclude that the problems lay in marketing, but this was not so, the main problems being a combination of poor quality and high production costs. This did not show in the accounting reports because parts were transferred between units at the full cost of production. It was only when the total cost of finished vehicles proved to be in excess of the price that could be obtained for them in the market place that the true loss became apparent. And even then it appeared in the accounts of the wrong division!

This is a good example of the danger of attempting to use accounting information beyond the limits of its validity. If operating units are interdependent no amount of accounting allocation will allow them to be controlled as if they were independent. Cost control is still possible, and should be used in conjunction with cost budgets, but the use of profit centres becomes highly suspect. Interdependence requires a high degree of coordination, and to pretend that decentralized control can be exercised *via* accounting reports is fallacious.

Impediments to the use of accounting information

Management accounting information concentrates on those aspects of control which are regular, and which depend on formally provided information about activities which are measurable in quantitative terms. However, this represents only part of the control process and informally derived information, often non-quantified and obtained sporadically, is at least as important. This may help explain the limited importance accorded to accounting information observed in a number of studies of information use by managers.

One such series of studies (Dew and Gee, 1973) focused on the use made of budgetary information by middle managers in manufacturing firms. The results indicated that only a small minority of managers made extensive use of the budgetary information provided to them; the vital pre-condition for use of budgetary information appeared to be participation (or minimally, consultation) in budget preparation. Thus many managers perceive the accounting information they receive as irrelevant to their needs, in part owing to their lack of involvement in its production.

Further light is thrown on the issue by the results of a subsequent study which asked managers at various hierarchical levels how they saw the primary purpose of cost accounting reports. Although the vast majority of senior managers stated that they saw the information as a control tool for the middle managers to use themselves, more than half the middle managers perceived its primary use as a means of measuring their own efficiency. There was thus a serious difference of opinion as to the purpose of the accounting information provided, with senior managers believing it to be useful to their subordinates, but many subordinates seeing it as only being of use to their superiors in monitoring their own behaviour. It is evidently important both to allow participation in budget preparation and to ensure that all levels of management are clear as to the function of accounting information in the organization. Nevertheless, such a duality of view is likely to prevail, as it reflects the partially conflicting interests of the parties involved.

Some other reasons for the lack of use made of formally provided management information were explored by Mintzberg (1975). He identified three main areas of concern: formal v informal information, organizational problems, and individual cognitive problems.

Formal and informal information systems were contrasted to identify why managers often prefer the latter, yielding four basic weaknesses of formal systems, namely:

1   The formal system can be too limited in that it is weak in supplying external information, and tends to ignore non-quantitative and non-economic information. For example, formal systems may report on sales made but they rarely report on sales lost.
2   Formal systems attempt to reduce information overload by aggregating data into bland totals and averages, rather than

reporting specific and tangible detail. Details of one complaint may be of more use to a manager when deciding what action to take than aggregate figures of the number of complaints received.

3 The formal system is often too slow; managers may need to act on rumours and grapevine information that arrives ahead of events, rather than reports that arrive after them.

4 Some formal information is unreliable, in the sense that what is reported does not convey the correct message.

A second set of problems arises from the organizational context in which the information is used. For example:

5 Rigid organizational objectives (e.g. output and profit targets) may encourage managers to meet the formal objectives by a variety of undesirable means.

6 The power structure and political structure within the organization may cause managers to ignore or distort information related to overall effectiveness. Budgetary bias and manipulation occur frequently in practice.

7 The nature of their work may encourage managers to favour verbal channels of communication and neglect documented sources.

Finally, individual cognitive limitations and personality factors can also effect information use in the following ways:

8 Cognitive limitations mean that only a very small amount of information can be properly assessed and appreciated at any one time. Appropriate selection of information is vital.

9 The brain filters information in line with previous patterns of experience, perhaps causing new information to be overlooked. Cyert et al. (1961) found that people extrapolated the same basic data differently depending on whether it was labelled 'costs' or 'revenues'. Costs were overestimated and revenues underestimated, perhaps due to an unconscious acknowledgement of the different impact of errors in each direction.

10 Psychological failures further impede the brain's openness to information. In particular, managers may filter out negative information once they have committed themselves to a given course of action.

In order to help overcome these impediments to the use of formally provided information, Mintzberg makes several recommendations, of which the more important are:

(a) Managers need broad-based formal information systems that include external information. The tendency towards computer-based information systems has been counter-productive in this respect.

(b) The information system needs to include intelligent filtering systems, more sophisticated than mere aggregation, to avoid the problems of information overload while allowing necessary detail to be accessed.

(c) The information system should have the capability of allowing in-depth search and encourage the use of multiple, possibly conflicting, sources of information. The manager needs different points of view and contrary opinions to counter his/her own mental prejudices.

(d) Appropriate channels of communication, geared to the manager's style of working, need to be developed.

Although some of the above recommendations go outside the scope of the accounting system, they do indicate the wider context in which accounting information is provided and used. Evidently, the most suitable conditions for effective budgetary control would include a stable operating environment, a well-defined organizational hierarchy with clearly specified responsibility centres and a minimum of interdependence with other parts of the organization. However, it might well be argued that if such conditions existed, then the need for budgetary control would be minimal! In practice external environments are changing, responsibilities overlap and what is controllable shades imperceptibly into what is not. It is perhaps not surprising that accounting control systems do not work perfectly and that they need to be designed individually for the specific circumstances facing a given organization. Nevertheless, the above analysis does give some indications of the directions in which accounting control systems need to develop in order to overcome their current limitations.

Conclusions

The provision of appropriate accounting information for planning, motivation and control involves both the setting of standards of performance (budgets) and reporting actual results for subunits within the organization. In this chapter we have identified some issues that result from the organizational context within which this process occurs. These include:

(a)   The conflict between the standards used for motivation and control, and those required in the planning process. Essentially two different sets of budgets are required for these two functions, although one of these is usually only informal.

(b)   The consequence of aggregating mildly optimistic budget targets up successive levels of the organizational hierarchy is that the aggregate target becomes absurdly difficult to achieve. One solution is to ensure that suitable amounts are deducted at each stage, to ensure that desired probabilities of attainment are preserved.

(c)   The lack of meaning in accounting profit and loss statements for interdependent operating units. Pseudo-profit centres are a hindrance, not an aid, to improved control.

(d)   The impediments to the effective use of accounting information in controlling activities which require the use of broader-based information. The accounting information system is part of a wider management information system and needs to be designed and used in conjunction with it.

· 7 ·

Budgetary
systems design

We have argued that the effective design and use of a budget system for management planning and control requires consideration of a wide range of individual and organizational factors. Previous chapters have dealt with these in some detail but, at the end of the day, a budget system has to be designed which is technically adequate to meet the range of demands placed upon it. In this chapter we therefore consider some of the technical problems which have to be resolved in setting up a budget system which can be used by managers to meet their control needs.

First, the basis of budget preparation is reviewed to establish the basic structure necessary for effective control. As the budget must serve multiple purposes, we next consider the specific needs of financial planning, short-term decision-making and management control. Finally, the ways in which the budget system can be adapted to meet situational differences are reviewed, using the contingency theory of management accounting as a guiding framework.

The basis of budget preparation

The technical processes involved in budget preparation are straightforward, if quite complex, and are well covered in many management accounting texts. An excellent exposition is given in the classic text by Edey (1966). However, it will be helpful to review the overall process here in order to clarify some of the assumptions that are necessarily made.

First, the process of budget preparation follows the organizational pattern of authority and responsibility. Overall budgets are built up from budgets for individual responsibility centres as defined by the organizational hierarchy. Typically the managers of these responsibility centres will have some influence over the content of the budget, although the degree of participation allowed can vary widely from organization to organization, and even within different parts of the same organization. But at least some consultation is usual, and a fuller participation up to almost total responsibility for the preparation of their own budget (with technical assistance from accounting staff) occurs in many organizations.

It is thus evident that the figures entered into the budget are the result of a bargaining process between a manager and his/her immediate superior, with a budget accountant possibly acting as an intermediary, in which the relative degree of influence of the parties can vary considerably. The lesser degree of formal power and authority of the junior manager relative to his/her superior is often more than compensated for by his/her greater degree of knowledge and understanding of the operation of the unit under his/her control. In general, the budget process is a means of reconciling the level of performance that is desired to meet overall corporate aims and constraints, with the performance that is feasible for the individual operating units. For the overall budget to be meaningful, it is essential that the results of this process represent similar standards of attainment for the various subunits involved.

Second, the organizational structure will largely determine whether responsibility centres will be treated as cost, revenue, profit or investment centres for the purpose of budgetary control, although some limited degree of discretion is possible. It is often suggested that managers should be held responsible only for those costs and revenues over which they exert significant influence. However, in practice it appears that a broader concept of responsibility is used, with managers being held accountable for their overall performance in relation to budget despite uncontrollable changes which have occurred.

Responsibility centres are most commonly cost or profit centres. Managers in charge of a cost centre are responsible for performing defined tasks (outputs) within a given cost budget (inputs). However, monetary values are assigned only to the inputs used and not to the outputs produced so their effectiveness, as distinct from their efficiency, has to be assessed using physical as well as accounting data. By contrast, managers of a profit centre are responsible for both costs (inputs) and revenues (outputs), and both their effectiveness and efficiency can be assessed using accounting data. The advantages of this latter arrangement are evident and the undoubted advantages of profit centres have led to their creation even when managers have only minimal influence over their reported revenues (i.e. pseudo-profit centres).

It may appear that the structure of organizational responsibilities determines the form of the budgetary control system, and indeed this is formally the case. But the reverse effect should not be overlooked, particularly from a longer term or strategic perspective. Organizations may adapt their responsibility structures so as to gain the advantages of profit centre accountability. In particular, divisional forms of organization can be seen as a relinquishment of detailed control by central management by the substitution of overall profit-based control. However, not only does such a divisional structure require giving subordinate managers a greater degree of autonomy and authority, it also raises the accounting issues of transfer pricing policy and the treatment of joint costs and revenues. But the main point to be made here is that the establishment of the budgetary control structure is part of an overall organizational design task; organizational structure and budgetary control system structure are mutually interdependent.

Third, budget preparation for operating activities is based directly upon standard costing. Although it may be possible to set an aggregate budget for a responsibility centre without a formal standard costing system, the ad hoc work involved makes it highly desirable that standard costing is implemented. A standard cost is a predetermined cost for the production of a unit of output, which may be further deemed to earn a standard price; the cost budget is the aggregate of all such standard costs, multiplied by planned output volumes, and supplemented by lump sum costs not related to volume of activity. Again, the technical process is straightforward (see Table 3), although it involves a very considerable amount of detailed work, but the fundamental problem involved relates to how the standard costs are derived.

Table 3 *Budget variance calculation*

A factory budgets to produce 1000 units of product and to sell them at £20 each. Standard costs of production amount to £17 per unit made up as follows:

		Unit cost £	Total cost £
Direct labour	2 hours @ £2 per hour	4.00	4,000
Direct materials	2 kg @ £3 per kg	6.00	6,000
Variable overhead	£1 per DLH	2.00	2,000
Fixed overhead	£5,000	5.00	5,000
Standard cost of production		17.00	17,000
Expected revenue		20.00	20,000
Standard profit margin		3.00	3,000

In fact 1200 units were produced and sold at an average price of £19 each. Actual costs of production amounted to £17.86 per unit made up as follows:

		Unit cost £	Total cost £
Direct labour	2.2 hours @ £1.90 per hour	4.18	5,016
Direct materials	1.9 kg @ £3.50 per kg	6.65	7,980
Variable overhead	£1.15 per DLH	2.53	3,036
Fixed overhead	£5,400	4.50	5,400
Actual cost of production		17.86	21,432
Actual revenue		19.00	22,800
Actual profit margin		1.86	1,368

The variance calculations must therefore show why the profit variance of £1,632 (U) (=£3,000 – £1,368) occurred. Note that as full costing is being employed, fixed overhead amounting to £6000 (i.e. 1200 units @ £5.00) has been absorbed rather than the £5000 originally budgeted, and standard profit is thus understated by £1000, explained by the £1000 over-absorbed overhead variance. This is best regarded as part of the volume variance, which can be defined as change in volume × standard contribution margin (i.e. 200 units × £8 = £1,600 (F)), rather than using standard profit margin.

The overall variance of £1,632 (U) can be explained as follows:

	Original budget 1000 units	Standard cost 1200 units	Flexible budget 1200 units	Actual costs	Variance
Direct labour cost	4,000	4,800	4,800	5,016	216 (U)
Direct materials cost	6,000	7,200	7,200	7,980	780 (U)
Variable overhead	2,000	2,400	2,400	3,036	636 (U)
Fixed overhead	5,000	6,000	5,000	5,400	400 (U)
Total costs	17,000	20,400	19,400	21,432	2,032 (U)
Revenue	20,000	24,000	24,000	22,800	1,200 (U)
Volume variance					600 (F)
Over-absorbed fixed o/h					1,000 (F)
Profit	3,000	3,600	4,600	1,368	1,632 (U)

However, for the purposes of reporting to management, the variances might be better categorized as follows:

(a) Volume variance due to higher production   1600 (F)
      (including accounting system variance)

(b) Efficiency variances

        Labour efficiency   480 (U)

        Materials usage   360 (F)

        Variable overhead efficiency   240 (U)

                              360 (U)

(c) Revenue and expense variances

        Selling price   1200 (U)

        Labour rate   264 (F)

        Materials price   1140 (U)

        Variable overhead rate   396 (U)

        Fixed overhead expense   400 (U)

                              2872 (U)

(d) Accounting system

      Fixed overhead absorption (if necessary)

        Total variances   1632 (U)

There are basically just two methods of determining standard costs. The first method involves the analysis of historical data; the standard cost then represents what has been achieved in the past, adjusted for any expected changes in efficiency and external economic factors such as price changes. The second method involves work measurement designed to measure the appropriate labour and material content of each product or service, and to cost it according-ly; the standard cost here represents a carefully assessed standard of attainment based on work study measurements. Although this may seem an objective procedure, it may not possess the degree of accuracy initially expected, as the necessary timings are made only with the knowledge of the workers involved. As the results of the exercise may also be used to set production standards or form the basis of a wage payment scheme, reliable timings may be hard to come by. Of course, work study officers are well aware of such problems but the process is not as objective as is sometimes supposed, and is fundamentally a process of bargaining in which both sides often appear well-matched.

Finally, it should be noted that budgets for profit centres require estimates of product prices and quantities expected to be sold. However, price setting, even in conditions of low uncertainty, requires information about market demands and production costs, and the process can become circular (i.e. price affects demand and thus production, which in turn affects costs and thus price). Costs themselves have an influence on optimal pricing policy. Great care needs to be taken to ensure that the assumptions made about the relationship between price and demand in constructing a budget are properly related to real market conditions and are not just arbitary formulae used for analytic convenience.

Budgets for financial planning

The processes of budget preparation considered in the previous section have related primarily to individual parts of the organiza-tion, considered more or less in isolation. We now turn to consider the overall coordination of activities, and in terms of both financial planning and management control. Finance is a major business function on a par with production, marketing and personnel; it is necessary for financial managers to have information about the plans of all major functions so that finance can be provided where necessary, but without waste of financial resources. By contrast, management control is the function of general managers, and is concerned with all aspects of coordination and integration within the organization. Nevertheless, much the same budget information can be used for both actitivies; indeed in diversified organizations general management operates primarily through financial control mechanisms. We shall therefore concern ourselves primarily with the use of budgets in financial planning in this section and go on to consider budgeting for management control in a later section.

The three main areas in which a budget can assist in financial planning relate to profitability, liquidity and asset structure, all of which affect the determination of overall financial structure. Profitability is of evident importance as it forms the substance of external financial information disclosure as well as providing an internal indication of success. Reported profits are likely to affect a company's share price, if only because the underlying cash flows and expected future cash flows are not public knowledge. Liquidity is a short-term constraint, but a vital one, for the consequences of running out of cash can be traumatic. Asset structure is a longer-term issue, but one which must be considered when overall financial structure is being planned. Budget statements in each of these three areas exactly match the equivalent reports of actual results, but using forecast and estimated figures rather than actuals. Thus budgeted profit and loss accounts, cash flow statements and balance sheets may be constructed, so that the financial outcomes of any set of plans can be predicted and assessed.

The process of constructing such budget statements however differs fundamentally from the production of actual financial reports. Whereas reports of actual results depend upon the combination of a large number of basic transactions, budget reports begin at the other end of the process and are based on a small number of overall assumptions and predictions. These assumptions are transmitted down to unit managers to enable them to produce their own unit budgets which are then aggregated to form an overall corporate budget. For financial planning purposes, even the involvement of middle line managers may be dispensed with, although it is absolutely essential that this involvement is retained for the purposes of management control.

Although budgeting is presented in accounting textbooks as an iterative technique whereby unacceptable outcomes are amended by revising the plans on which they are based, in practice the sheer time and tedium involved in budget recalculation generally leads to a very few alternatives being considered. However, the advent of computerized systems has now produced a situation where a great deal of useful exploration can be conducted using a budget model. Spreadsheet programs, or the more sophisticated financial planning models now available, enable the consequences of many different plans to be quickly assessed once the basic budget model for the organization has been developed.

At the technical level the procedure is logical, if complex, and a good practical guide is contained in Sherwood (1983). Once estimates of the necessary factors have been made, a simple budget model can be built in a few hours and even a relatively complex model for a sizable organization constructed in a few man-months. The major difficulty lies in estimating the relationships that exist between variables. For example, what proportion of production costs are variable with output, and over what range does this relationship hold? At what point do overtime rates become payable and how much overtime is feasible? What are the capacity limitations on the plant? What is the relationship between advertising expenditure and sales? And so on. A very great deal of detailed analysis generally has to be done, even where standard cost and variable cost systems are currently implemented.

Financial planning packages are usually set up in a way that helps these problems to be coped with. Most can have many years of historical data entered into them, and allow the modeller to analyse the relationships that seem to have existed in the past, and to project these as forecasts into the future. Nevertheless the provision of accurate predictions of future consequences is a demanding and time-consuming task, requiring a good knowledge of the operations of all parts of the organization. However, as the validity of the budget model depends totally on the accuracy of the relationships that are incorporated into it, it is essential that these are properly analysed and validated. Inevitably some estimates will come directly from the line managers most closely concerned with particular operations, as they are often in the best position to predict what is likely to happen. This is a quite reasonable procedure, but can prove to be dangerous if these estimates are subsequently altered by the planner without making the necessary consequential changes because knowledge of these consequences existed only in the mind of the manager, not having been incorporated into the formal model.

There is no doubt that computer-based financial planning models provide a powerful tool that enable senior managers to explore the consequences of a much wider range of plans than was possible in the past, and thus to arrive at better plans, if only because of the greater range of alternatives considered. But it must always be remembered that a model is only as good as the assumptions about relationships on which it is based. The role of the budget accountant in providing managers with financial models of their operations, so that they can jointly explore the consequences of alternative possibilities, is likely to be increasingly important in the future.

However, it must also be emphasized that financial planning is only part of the overall management control process. Although the financial models described here are of considerable use in the development of overall strategic plans for the organization as a whole, they are not a substitute for the detailed involvement of all levels of line management in the construction of budget estimates to which they will subsequently be held accountable. Overall financial planning is a preliminary stage in that process; it must be followed by the careful establishment of detailed budgets acceptable to managers at all levels.

Budgets and decision-making

The construction of budgets, typically for a period of a year ahead, is intimately bound up with short-term decision-making. Typical short-term decisions include setting output levels, choosing a product mix, fixing inventory levels and deciding on a pricing policy. Assumptions about all these matters need to be made in the process of budget construction and, once a budget has been fixed, these decisions may limit managerial discretion throughout the budget period. Thus, the time at which the budget is set is also the time at which a large number of short-term operating decisions have to be made. This is not to imply that such decisions cannot be subject to change during the budget period; they frequently are changed and this often requires amendment to the budgets. Rather, setting budgets automatically requires a wide range of short-term operating decisions to be made, albeit tentatively.

The central accounting concept necessary for evaluating short-term decisions is that of variable cost. Variable costs are defined as those which change in proportion to output, in contrast to fixed costs which remain constant over a range of different output levels. Traditionally, cost items such as materials and direct labour have been considered variable, although the impact of trades unions and employment legislation has made this less valid. Most cost and management accounting texts go into considerable detail with regard to how fixed and variable costs should be estimated, and how the distinction can be made more sophisticated by defining step function fixed costs and several different variable cost rates applicable at different levels of activity. In such ways, accounting data can be used to operationalize the economic idea of marginal analysis, although it is notable that much less attention has been paid to the estimation of price-demand relationships.

However, the distinction between fixed and variable costs depends crucially on the time horizon of the decision being considered. In the very short term nearly all costs are fixed; in the long term all costs become variable. Thus a particular split between fixed and variable costs is valid only for one particular time horizon of decision. The analysis conducted for budget purposes may well be different to that conducted for other purposes, although perhaps what needs to be emphasized is that such a cost analysis is absolutely necessary. A budget constructed without a clear understanding of cost behaviour patterns is useless. A second major problem in cost analysis is the allocation of joint costs to particular products or operating units. Generally, this can be avoided in financial planning, although it may be necessary in setting control budgets for managers (Emmanuel and Otley, 1985).

The problem is particularly acute for companies that do not prepare variable cost information on a routine basis, and rely solely on full cost statements, perhaps in part because of the difficulty in establishing reliable variable cost data. Not only is the process of budgeting made more difficult without comparable past actual figures being available, but it is very easy for managers to fall into the trap of treating the profit figures as being valid for all decisions, regardless of the impact of changes in the level of output. It is all too common to see senior managers run their fingers down a list of product profit figures and demand instant action whenever they encounter a product showing a loss.

Both full and variable cost statements contain valuable information that, if interpreted correctly, can give guidance to the decision maker. Whereas the variable cost information can be used to predict the short-term impact of decisions, the full cost information is more relevant to the prediction of longer-term impact. When profit figures based on full-cost accounting are the major summary measure of performance, it is especially important not to interpret them in inappropriate ways. However, it would be better if variable cost accounting statements and contribution figures were to be produced on a routine basis together with the full cost information. Budgeting cannot sensibly proceed without the necessary analysis being conducted, and a great deal of useful information is lost if actual cost information is not also collected in this form.

Budgets for management control

The major difference in using budgets for management control rather than just financial planning, is that line managers at all levels must be involved. Whereas financial planning can be carried out by specialist staff making their own estimates of likely outcomes and producing their own financial plan, this is not an adequate procedure when the budget is intended to be used for management control. In addition, the types of estimate entered into the budget will differ. In financial planning what is required is a best estimate of anticipated outcomes, or possibly a conservative estimate of cash flow such that there is the smallest possible chance of the organization becoming illiquid. By contrast, for management control purposes, the budget will be used as a means of motivating, controlling and evaluating the performance of line managers, and requires to be set in a manner that is consistent with these purposes.

The only way to ensure that a budget is accepted by a line manager as a reasonable standard against which his/her future performance is to be assessed is to allow him/her to participate in the budget-setting process. This is not to imply that subordinate managers should have the sole right to determine the content of their own budget, but rather that the content should be discussed with them and the budget set in a way that takes their views into account. There is no doubt that there will always be considerable differences in the relative influence that superiors and subordinates have on the setting of budgets. Some of these are quite rational; for example, one would expect that an experienced superior dealing with a newly-appointed subordinate would exert more influence than when the superior is newly-appointed and the subordinate has many years of experience. However, on other occasions, relative influence may be affected by the personalities of the two managers involved, the degree of budget pressure being exerted by senior management, and the overall financial and competitive state of the organization as a whole.

Nor do the junior managers necessarily have to be specifically involved in many of the financial aspects of budget-setting. In many circumstances their contribution may lie primarily in the specification of the technical and operating standards that are feasible and appropriate, leaving it to others to spell out the financial implications of such standards. Nevertheless, regardless of how it is achieved, the participation of line managers in providing the basic information on which their budget is set is essential if the budget is to act as an effective motivational device that they set their sights on attaining.

The *level* at which standards are set has an effect upon actual performance, as outlined in Chapter 4, but the *process* by which they are set is likely to be even more influential. Managers who feel that their views have been taken fully into account in setting their budget, and who know that their subsequent performance will be evaluated against that budget, are far more likely to be positively motivated to perform well than managers who feel that they have been ignored or over-ridden without explanation. Nevertheless, it must be recognized that budget-setting is essentially a bargaining process, and one which is affected by the relative power of the two parties involved. Because superiors have the great formal power, it is wise for them to be particularly careful in not appearing to impose their views on their subordinates without full discussion.

The process of budgeting has been described as a 'game' (Hofstede, 1968), in that it appears to work most effectively when the participants are relatively evenly matched and it is not taken *too* seriously. Budgets are only partial and imperfect means of assisting in obtaining good performance, and should not be taken over-seriously. But, as Hofstede comments:

> In stressing the game element of budgeting, let me make it clear that I do not want to do away with control . . . Now the basic problem is how budgeting can be considered a game, because it is part of a formal, purposeful control system, and should remain part of it. However, the answer is that this control system has repeatedly proven to be self-destroying when used in a direct, mechanical way. It is so complicated because of all the technological, economic and human elements involved that in a mathematical sense its operation is 'over-determined' – like five equations with four unknowns. In order to make it viable, a 'play' or margin or tolerance or random element must be introduced into the system, and this is the condition that makes it possible to exercise budget control as a game.

To continue the analogy, budgeting is a game in two parts, perhaps most similar to bridge. In the bidding phase the budget standard is set; this is followed by a playing phase in which the standard is attempted to be achieved. Further, one cycle of play is followed by another, and lessons learnt in the previous period of play can be used in subsequent periods. However, care needs to be taken to ensure that effort is devoted to achieving the standard rather than being spent in unproductive competition with other players. Too great a stress on comparative performance can lead both to the manipulation of accounting information, undesirable behaviour and attempts to reduce the reported performance of other units in the organization (Hopwood, 1972). Meeting the budget should be important, but not *too* important.

Budget variances

Once a budget has been set, actual performance is regularly reported, compared with the budget target, and accounting variances are calculated. Such variances are of four main types, with different action being needed in each case:

1   *Volume* variances occur when actual output has differed from that budgeted. For the monetary figure reported to give a true

reflection of actual performance it is essential that the amount of a volume variance is calculated on a contribution basis using variable costs, otherwise considerable distortions can occur because the true volume variance is confounded with an accounting system variance (e.g. under- or over-absorption of fixed costs). Normally, overspending on account of volume changes is regarded as an acceptable, or even a good occurrence. After all, it indicates that more has been produced than was expected, and the marginal cost of such production is usually low. However, it may upset product-mix requirements, and also cause increased inventory holding costs as well as having liquidity consequences. In non-profit organizations which do not sell their product to the final consumer (e.g. nationalized health care services) volume variances indicate that more goods or services have been supplied than was planned for, but that increased expenditure was necessary to provide them. Cash limits have been a recently emphasized device to limit such over-provision of government funded services. In both cases, however, the volume variance needs to be calculated in order to distinguish it from efficiency variances.

2 *Efficiency* variances indicate the amount of inputs used (in physical terms, because inputs are valued at their standard cost) in producing the given output. Thus an adverse efficiency variance indicates that the technical standards allowed for the conversion of inputs into outputs have not been met. The responsibility for such variances is usually clearly that of the line manager concerned, as it represents items such as materials wastage or the inefficient use of available labour.

3 *Expense* variances indicate whether inputs have been acquired at the standard costs allowed (e.g. materials price variance, labour rate variance) or ouputs sold at the expected prices (product price variance). They also include fixed cost variances when sums other than those budgeted have been paid for items having their own lump sum budget (e.g. factory rent and rates). Such variances may be the responsibility of the line manager concerned, although there is often a substantial external influence. For example, material prices may be the responsibility of a purchasing manager, and in any case are affected by external factors quite beyond the control of the organization. Care

therefore needs to be taken in assigning responsibility for such variances.

4 *Accounting* system variances are those that are caused purely by the accounting policies of the organization. An example would be a fixed overhead 'volume' variance, indicating that changes in production volume had caused fixed overheads to be under- or over-absorbed (under a full-costing system). Such variances are not the responsibility of line managers, as they have no control of them, and they should be excluded completely from their performance appraisal.

It is important for variances to be separated into these categories, as the appropriate action that should be taken is different in each case, as indicated in the numerical example given in Table 3. Volume variances indicate the need for revised production planning, or for further controls to be placed on output levels. Efficiency variances indicate that internal performance standards have not been met, whereas expense variances are usually more affected by external factors. Accounting system variances concern nobody but the finance staff, unless they are required to adjust volume or efficiency variances that have not previously been calculated on an appropriate basis. It should be noted that the separation of volume, efficiency and accounting variances requires that a flexible budgeting system based on variable costs is installed, otherwise the figures produced do not relate to any single category, and control thus becomes confounded.

The reaction of senior managers to budget variances is also important. Too great a pressure on achieving budget targets can be counter productive, as indicated in Chapter 4. The art of budget control appears to lie in applying just enough pressure to ensure that meeting the budget is recognized to be important, but not so much as to make it the be all and end all of managerial activity. Finally, the most important use of budget variances is that they should be used to assist managers to learn from their past mistakes so that future performance is improved.

The contingency theory of management accounting

So far the recommendations for budget systems design have been couched in general terms as if they were applicable to organizations of all types. But there is an increasing amount of evidence that many aspects of budgetary control are dependent upon the specific circumstances in which the organisation exists. The contingency theory of management accounting has attempted to analyse how specific differences in circumstances affect accounting information system design.

The contingency theory of management accounting seeks to provide a rationale for the design of accounting information systems. It attempts to categorize accounting information systems into different types, and to explain the occurrence of each type of system by identifying appropriate contingent variables. By drawing on insights from organization theory it provides a framework for an integrated theory of management accounting set in its organizational context. As Sathe (1980) hopefully stated:

> Future research will benefit if management accounting were viewed not so much as a separate and distinct area of knowledge but rather as being reciprocally interdependent with the general field of organization theory.

Three main classes of explanatory variables have been identified: environment, organizational structure and technology. Environment is typically ill-defined and covers factors as diverse as uncertainty, heterogeneity of product-markets, market dynamism and competitive hostility. Organizational structure is treated as an independent variable, with little recognition that it is reciprocally interdependent with the overall management information and control system. Technology is loosely related to the production process in general, and to task uncertainty in particular (Otley, 1980). For example, it has been suggested that organizations operating in an uncertain environment will develop accounting systems that frequently monitor the key areas affected by uncertainty. Similarly, in a highly competitive market, accounting information on competitors will be sought and used to model their likely responses to marketing initiatives. Further, organizations that are highly interdependent internally have been shown to use budgetary control information less rigidly in performance evaluation than those which are composed of virtually independent parts. Finally, differences in production technology affect accounting information systems design, as in the differences between job and process costing systems.

There is no doubt that differences in environment, structure and technology do have an important influence on accounting systems design in general, and on budgetary control systems design in particular, but there is little hard evidence on exactly what that influence is in specific terms. The size of an organization also affects the degree to which the replacement of personal controls by more formal, accounting controls is necessary. There is a need to establish a theoretically coherent set of categories to characterize management accounting systems; that is, to identify what features of a management accounting system are expected to be related to various contingent variables. It is significant that one of the earliest articles (Gordon and Miller, 1976) still remains one of the best introductions to the topic, particularly with respect to its emphasis on the precise impact of the contingent variables on various features of the accounting information system.

However, contingency theory does not yet appear to have fulfilled its early promise. The conceptual basis of contingency theory is still little more than a mêlée of theoretical ideas tested by somewhat inappropriate research methodologies. Although some potentially relevant contingent variables have been identified, little work has been done on defining how accounting systems should be adapted due to such differences.

More recently, the emphasis in contingency theory research has moved away from surveys that aim to be representative and to produce general results, towards more restricted studies which give insight into particular issues. In what is perhaps the most significant recent study, Jones (1985) chose to study the accounting systems of companies that had recently merged or had been taken over. By comparing the pre- and post-acquisition accounting systems of both the acquiring and acquired companies, he demonstrated the dominating effect of consistency with the acquiring company's accounting principles. In many cases, the more traditional contingent variables had little impact compared with the desire for standardization. The management accounting system of acquired companies was required to conform to standard, centrally-imposed patterns, although some flexibility was permitted in the operational control techniques utilized. This study therefore suggests at least two new contingent variables namely ownership and corporate financial accounting practice. It may also be considered to show that contingency theory is itself inadequate, certainly for business units that are owned by larger entities.

Despite these problems the contingency framework is valuable, but there is a need for researchers to be more specific about the contingent variables being considered and to pay more attention to defining the dimensions of the accounting system that are thought to be affected by these variables. Contingency theory should not be expected ever to provide a total design prescription, but it probably is capable of providing significant insight into the major design contingencies. The budgetary control systems designer should therefore be aware of developments in this field.

Conclusions

Budget systems design is not just a technical accounting exercise, but has important connections with the overall management and control of the organization. Budgetary control structure and organizational design are closely interconnected, and in the long term should be considered in conjunction. In the short term budgetary control structure follows from organizational structure, and some guiding principles include:

(a) Effective budgetary control requires profit centres to be established only where managers have a clear responsibility for both costs and revenues.
(b) Variable costing is essential to effective budgetary control if changes in volume can occur.
(c) Standard costing is a highly desirable adjunct to a budgetary control system, and requires little extra work to implement.
(d) The effects of pricing policy need to be incorporated into a complete budget model.
(e) The involvement of line managers in budget-setting is essential for effective use of budgets in management control.

(f)   Senior managers should take great care not to unnecessarily impose budgets on their subordinates.

(g)   Variances should be analysed into volume, efficiency, expense and accounting system components, with responsibility for each variance being assigned to the most appropriate managers.

· 8 ·

Capital
budgeting

Previous chapters have been primarily concerned with the construction and use of operating budgets that are generally constructed for a period of a year or so, and initially based on the assumption that existing plant and equipment will be retained. However, planned changes in fixed assets are of vital importance to the continued well-being of an organization, and such changes involve the spending of money now in the expectation of obtaining returns over a number of years. Because the time horizon of such investment decisions exceeds the time horizon of the operating budget, it is necessary to have separate procedures for the evaluation of proposed capital investments.

We shall first consider the main stages in the capital budgeting process, and note that relatively little academic attention has been paid to any of these stages except that of evaluation. Typically, it is recommended that project evaluation should be performed on a discounted cash flow (DCF) basis by calculating the net present value (NPV) of expected cash flows at some selected discount rate. Therefore the problems of choosing an appropriate discount rate and of evaluating proposed investments under conditions of uncertainty will be discussed next. Finally, the potential conflict between taking investment decisions based on a DCF analysis but subsequently evaluating performance using accounting profit and return on investment (RoI) figures, will be demonstrated and possible methods of avoiding the problem outlined.

Stages in the capital budgeting process

The capital budgeting process may be regarded as being comprised of six stages (King, 1975):

1 Project origination.
2 Estimation of expected cash flows.
3 Progress of the proposal through the organization.
4 Evaluation of proposals.
5 Authorization of expenditure.
6 Post-audit investigations.

It has been suggested that the evaluation stage has pre-occupied academic discussion to the neglect of other stages (Pinches, 1982) although this misplaced emphasis is gradually being rectified in the literature. We shall therefore examine each stage in turn.

Project origination

Although we shall talk about capital investment decisions in general terms, there are in fact many different types of decision that have capital expenditure implications. These range from the essential replacement of major items of equipment that can no longer be adequately maintained, through proposals to make desirable improvements that are expected to lead to substantial cost savings or the generation of new revenues, to full-blown new projects separate from existing activities. In addition, there are normal operating decisions that have capital implications, such as the decision to increase batch sizes, which can lead to additional capital being required to finance larger inventories, and also non-productive investments, such as spending on employee welfare services, that cannot be evaluated directly on cash flow based criteria.

The need for many of the above types of project often first becomes evident at lower levels in the organization. Very often it is the operating manager who is most aware of the need to invest more capital in production facilities. Thus the vital first stage in the progress of a capital investment proposal is for a project to be identified and to emerge from lower levels in the organization, and it is here that the first filtering takes place. Some projects, which might eventually have been considered to be highly desirable by senior management, never see the light of day because they do not appeal to the managers who first thought of them. For example, they see the proposal as being more risky than they wish to undertake, or as involving additional effort for which they do not have time to spare. They may also calculate that the replacement of old plant having a low book value by new plant of high value will adversely affect their reported profits and RoI. It is therefore likely that some good projects will never get brought to the attention of senior managers, and that some potentially profitable investment opportunities will be filtered out at lower levels.

These views are substantiated by a number of research studies. King (1975) observed that investment proposals involve a great deal of work for the originator, and are accompanied by a high level of personal risk with little tangible reward. Berg (1965) also noted that risky projects were frequently not proposed, even though the risk could be diversified and substantially reduced when placed in the context of the company as a whole, and similar conclusions were reached both by Aharoni (1966) and Carter (1971). This is a particularly severe problem for the diversified firm, where senior management are heavily reliant on divisional management to originate projects due to their superior knowledge of the product market (Ackerman, 1970).

It therefore appears that lower level managers can exercise substantial choice in deciding which projects to submit into the formal capital budgeting process. The constraints imposed by top management by the corporate plan and constraints on allocated expenditure may place limits on lower management's discretion, but the negative choice of not submitting a potential project will always be open.

Estimation of expected cash flows

In general terms, it is likely that lower level managers will only submit projects that they believe will have a good chance of acceptance. There is little point in undertaking the work of project submission if the project is not thought to have a good chance of success. Further, to have sponsored an unsuccessful project may be regarded as a black mark on a manager's performance record. In addition, several of the studies referenced above found evidence that project originators biased information to make their proposals look more attractive.

It can be argued that the project originator is best placed to provide information about likely outcomes, given his/her intimate knowledge of the product, market and technology involved. However, Bower (1971) regarded the central problem of capital investment appraisal as that of disentangling the forecasts of financial information from the personal commitment of the project sponsor. Tying rewards to the difference between results and forecasts may produce downward bias, whereas not rewarding results may induce optimistic bias in exactly the same way as has been noted in operating budgets (Chapter 5). In capital budgeting however, the time between making the forecasts and observing the outcomes is considerably longer than in operating budgeting, giving greater opportunity for bias.

Thus senior managers will observe that all of the projects submitted to them apparently meet the criteria for acceptance that they have previously laid down. The first stage in project evaluation must therefore be to weed out those projects that appear acceptable only because of the inflated cash flow estimates that have been incorporated into them. This can be a time-consuming task and require the services of a capital investment appraisal support group in a large organisation, charged with the responsibility of making a detailed assessment of all capital investment proposals put forward.

Progress of the proposal through the organization

Although some capital expenditure decisions can be made at lower levels in the organization, proposals involving expenditure greater than some, typically very modest, amount have to be approved by top management. This is undoubtedly because of the long-term influence of capital expenditure decisions and the need to ensure that they are consistent with overall corporate plans. Studies indicate that, as a project passes through an organization, the changing commitment of different groups to it has an influence on its eventual acceptance.

Aharoni (1966) argues that there is no one investment decision made at a single point in time, but instead a long process involving many people at different organizational levels. The collection of information necessitates contact with other parts of the firm, the revision of subjective estimates and the exchange of tacit promises of support. The accumulation of commitments limits the freedom of action available in subsequent stages of the evaluation procedures until an almost inevitable decision is reached. Strong commitment, especially from the project's originator, is required in order to devote the time necessary to extract promises of support. The project's upward progress through the organization is therefore a political process in which the originator is continually seeking higher level sponsors.

Evaluation of proposals

It is widely accepted that capital investment proposals should be evaluated by DCF techniques. However, managerial performance is most often measured in terms of a rate of return on investment (RoI) or profit before interest and tax (Scapens *et al.*' 1982). Typically, any incentive scheme operated by the firm is also based on these accounting performance measures, which means that the manger who submits a project because of its acceptable NPV, but who ignores its effect on profit and RoI, may be disadvantaged.

Where such an inconsistency occurs, the originating manager has a further reason for filtering out the project before it gets into the formal appraisal process. Only projects that have *both* acceptable NPVs (or internal rate of returns (IRRs)) *and* acceptable accounting profits (or RoIs) will be allowed to go forward. This is an important effect and will be discussed at greater length in the next section.

A similar effect may occur at senior levels. Despite a project being acceptable according to DCF criteria, senior management may judge that the lack of accounting profits in early years make it unacceptable to the firm, which may be evaluated by the stock market on the basis of current profits rather than promised future profits. A further constraint may be imposed by liquidity requirements. Although in theory these may be met by external financing, in practice this may be difficult to obtain. Thus, although the maximization of NPV may be the only criterion used in simple theories, in practice the pattern of cash flows, accounting profits and returns on investment for a portfolio of projects may also have a significant influence on project selection.

There is also some interesting evidence (Klammer, 1983) that indicates that companies who use the more sophisticated methods of capital investment appraisal (e.g. NPV and IRR) obtain significantly poorer performance than those who use cruder methods (e.g. payback period, accounting rate of return). This counter-intuitive result is most probably explained by the fact that companies which have a good supply of acceptable projects do not require sophisticated selection techniques to choose which to undertake. However, companies with only marginal projects have to take great care to ensure they undertake only those which will in fact prove to be beneficial. Appraisal methods are perhaps considerably less important than methods that encourage project generation.

Authorization of expenditure

The overwhelming impression given by empirical studies is that final authorization of capital expenditure decisions is purely 'rubber-stamping'. Capital investment proposals that reach the stage of formal application for authorization by top management are very rarely turned down, because the true selection is made informally, lower down the organization. By the time authorization is requested, the acceptability of the project to the originator and a large section of the organization has been determined. The authorization stage may therefore be regarded as a monitoring device to ensure that the project has undergone the normal planning procedures. However it must be open to serious doubt as to whether it is capable of preventing opportunistic behaviour by lower level managers at the earlier stages of origination, estimation of cash flows or selection.

Post-audit

The purpose of a post-audit is to compare some of the project outcomes with the original estimates, and it is usually undertaken after the project has been implemented and operated for a short period, although it is by no means a universally adopted procedure (Scapens et al., 1982). However, when it is used, it appears to be operated in an enlightened manner as a learning device to improve future estimates rather than as a means of criticizing those who made the original estimates. It must be recognized that it is often difficult to ascertain whether estimates were in fact achieved, particularly for those projects which form part of an integrated manufacturing process where cash flows due specifically to the investment cannot necessarily be identified.

Consideration of all six stages in the progress of a capital investment proposal indicates that capital budgeting is an even more complex process than operating budgeting, requiring careful handling to obtain an acceptable balance between encouraging the submission of new projects, but accepting only those having a good chance of success. The time horizons involved make risk and uncertainty play a crucial role in this process and require their consideration in a separate section.

Risk and uncertainty

All decisions involve risk because the future is inherently uncertain. However, risk is a major factor in capital investment appraisal because of the long-time horizons involved, and some means of taking it formally into account is required. The most common method of allowing for risk in DCF analysis is to increase the discount rate (or the required IRR target) for the more risky projects. Thus, in a divisionalized firm, divisions facing the more uncertain environments would be required to show a higher projected return from their investment projects than divisions facing a more stable environment, to compensate for the greater probability of those returns not being achieved.

Nevertheless, such a procedure has two problems. First there is the question of how the amount of the increase in the discount rate is to be assessed, and whether it should differ not only between divisions, but also between projects of different risk within the same division. Second, increasingly the discount rate to take account of risk carries with it the implicit assumption that risk increases exponentially with time. Although this may be valid for some projects, it is certainly erroneous for others. For example, a project such as the launch of a new product may be initially highly risky, but within a short time it will become apparent whether it is a success or a total failure. If the product proves to be initially successful, from then on returns may be assured and it carries little further risk. In these circumstances an increase in the discount rate may not be the most appropriate way of proceeding.

An alternative method of analysis has been put forward by Hertz (1964). He suggests that discounting should be used only where its validity is unquestioned; that is, in putting cash flows, known with certainty to occur at different points of time, into equivalent terms. The estimated cash flows for a project should therefore be discounted at the risk-free cost of capital, and risk taken into account in an alternative manner. The method suggested by Hertz involves estimating a probability distribution for each year's cash flows and combining these (using Monte Carlo simulation techniques) into a probability distribution for NPV. The result of such an analysis is shown in the diagram in Figure 3.

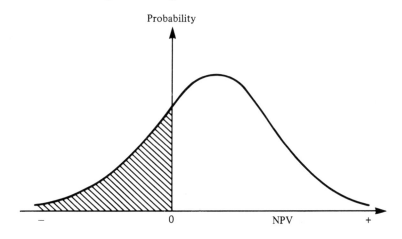

Figure 3 *Probability distribution of NPV*

From such a graph the likelihood of any NPV occuring can be assessed. Thus the shaded area to the left of the probability axis represents the likelihood that the project will not attain a positive NPV. Hertz argues that such a graph should be presented to senior management, in place of the single point estimates of NPV and IRR currently provided, to enable them to assess the risk involved against the potential returns. This involves them in subjective judgment, but might be preferable to presenting figures of expected NPV having a spurious air of objectivity, but which are in fact based on dubious assumptions.

Surveys of capital investment practice (Lister, 1984 reviews these) have shown that companies use a wide variety of measures in evaluating investment proposals. Many organizations have proposal documents that require not only DCF information, such as NPV and IRR, but also accounting rates of return and payback period. Such a battery of measures may be seen as one way of taking both multiple criteria (e.g. NPV, RoI and liquidity) and the riskiness of returns into account. It is evidently important to give senior managers a wide range of information about projects on which to base their decisions. Inevitably, capital investment appraisal involves subjective judgment as well as more objective and quantifiable information.

Conflict between project appraisal and performance appraisal

Regardless of how risk and uncertainty are treated, capital budgeting theory is quite clear on one issue. Projects should be evaluated on the basis of the NPV of their expected future cash flows. However, managerial performance is typically not evaluated by reference to cash flows, but in terms of the level of profit achieved or the return on investment attained. It will be shown that there can be a clear conflict between the measures used to appraise a capital investment project and those subsequently used to evaluate managerial performance. Thus, managers may well be motivated not to undertake desirable projects (according to NPV criteria) because the addition of such projects would adversely affect their own performance measures.

We shall show this by means of a simple numerical example, outlined in Table 4. Suppose we have three alternative capital investment projects available to us (X, Y and Z) each involving an initial investment of £1,200, and that the expected cash inflows from each project are those shown in Table 4. For the sake of simplicity, let us also suppose that these inflows are known with certainty, so that it is appropriate to discount these cash flows at the risk-free cost of capital, here assumed to be 10 per cent.

Table 4 *Cash flows for three alternative projects*

	Project X £	Project Y £	Project Z £
Initial investment	(1200)	(1200)	(1200)
Cash inflow at end of 1st year	500	500	200
Cash inflow at end of 2nd year	500	300	700
Cash inflow at end of 3rd year	500	600	700
Net present value @ 10% discount	43	(47)	86
Internal rate of return	12.04%	7.84%	13.43%

It can clearly be seen that on both NPV and DCF criteria project Z is the best. Project X is also acceptable, whereas project Y is undesirable. However, if the projects were to be accepted, the accounting figures that would be reported are shown in Tables 5 and 6. Here, project Z shows a loss of £200 in the first year and an RoI of – 16.7 per cent. Thus it is quite likely that managers who are concerned about their current performance would be unwilling to take on such a project because of its adverse affect on their reported results. It should also be noted that projects X and Y appear to be identical in the first year of operation, despite one being acceptable and the other not. Further, although project X has identical cash inflows in each of the three years, its reported return on investment increases dramatically due to the reducing net asset value of the investment.

Table 5   *Reported profits for three alternative projects (using straight line depreciation)*

	Project X £	Project Y £	Project Z £
Year 1	100	100	(200)
Year 2	100	(100)	300
Year 3	100	200	300

Table 6   *Return on investment for three alternative projects (using opening book value as the investment base)*

	Project X	Project Y	Project Z
Year 1	8.3%	8.3%	(16.7%)
Year 2	12.5%	(12.5%)	87.5%
Year 3	25.0%	50.0%	175.0%

It is sometimes suggested that residual income (RI) provides a means of mitigating the conflict described above, and to a certain extent this is true. Table 7 shows the residual income (accounting profit less a charge for capital employed, calculated here as the net asset value multiplied by the cost of capital) for each of the three projects. Now project Y is evidently not desirable, but project Z still appears in a poor light in the first year. Indeed both acceptable projects have negative RIs in the first year. This is a consequence of the depreciation method used, and can be partly overcome by the use of annuity depreciation. The results of such an analysis are given in Table 8, where it can be seen that different positive profit figures are now reported in each of the first three years. However, unless one values an asset at the NPV of its future expected cash flows (an unacceptable accounting procedure for most purposes) it does not achieve the desired result for projects having unequal cash flows, such as projects Y or Z.

Table 7 *Residual income for three alternative projects (using straight line depreciation and 10 per cent discount rate)*

	Project X £	Project Y £	Project Z £
Year 1	(20)	(20)	(320)
Year 2	20	(180)	220
Year 3	60	160	260
Present value of residual income	43	(47)	86

Table 8 *Profits for project X using annuity depreciation*

	Time period	Value of future cash flows	Depreci- ation	Cash flow	Profit	RoI
Now		1243				
	Year 1		375	500	125	10%
End of year 1		868				
	Year 2		413	500	87	10%
End of year 2		455				
	Year 3		455	500	45	10%
End of year 3		0				

It is evident that there is a fundamental conflict between NPV methods of project appraisal and normal accounting methods of performance measurement, including RI. Managers who are concerned about how their performance will be evaluated may well be motivated not to put forward projects with positive NPVs, but which show poor accounting profits in the early years of their life. The central cause of this conflict lies in the use of depreciation according to usual accounting principles. Perhaps we should therefore consider a system of performance measurement that does not involve depreciation (and other arbitary cost allocations).

Henderson and Dearden (1966) provide possibly the best suggestion for integrating capital and operating budgeting systems. Their proposal for cash flow accounting focuses on the integration of three budgets. The first is a contribution budget consisting of the expected revenues less variable operating costs. They suggest that this budget is prepared annually, with comparisons with actual costs being made monthly. The other two budgets, a fixed cost budget and a capital budget, would be used to feed information into the contribution budget. Only cash costs are included in both these latter two budgets, with depreciation and other costs representing allocations from previous decisions being excluded. However, when decisions are taken which change current operations, the promised future cash flows are included in the appropriate year's contribution budget. Similarly, the cash flows on which a capital investment proposal is justified are also included in the contribution budget.

As with all proposals for the improvement of budgetary systems, this suggestion has its drawbacks. First, the manager responsible for the contribution budget may have little incentive to divest him/her self of unused assets. The investment base of the division affects the contribution budget only indirectly by determining the capacity available to generate revenues. Second, where transfer pricing is involved, the manager working to a contribution budget may try to inflate expected revenue, or may not attempt to improve efficiency if a standard cost base is used. Finally, it assumes performance is measured in absolute terms of profit or contribution, rather than in the more common ratio terms, such as RoI. However, in favour of the integrated cash flow budget it may be argued that it does use the same measures both to appraise capital investment proposals and to evaluate managerial performance, both measures being based on cash flows. Perhaps the use of a wider range of performance measures, including both cash flow and more traditional accounting figures, provides a constructive way forward.

Conclusions

Capital budgeting raises many of the same issues as operating budgeting, although often in a more acute form. Managers may bias the information they put into the budget process, and in capital budgeting there is a greater period that will elapse before a comparison between budget and actual can be made. Indeed, in many cases, cash flows cannot be uniquely identified with a particular investment, so a formal appraisal of estimate accuracy cannot be undertaken.

However, the most important part of the capital budgeting process is not the appraisal of proposed investments, for which a range of accounting procedures exist and which are well-understood, but the generation of capital projects worth undertaking. These are often in short supply and it is vital that their number is not reduced by managers failing to put forward proposals because they have an adverse impact on immediate accounting income or RoI. Some progress in this direction might be made by ensuring that a wider range of measures was used to assess managerial performance, such as cash flow budgets, and perhaps encouraging the submission of projects rather than the discouraging approach that often exists at present. Capital rationing may make it inevitable that only a proportion of projects can be implemented, but managers can be rewarded for putting forward good ideas, even if it does not prove possible to act on them immediately.

Capital investment also involves a greater degree of risk than operating budgeting, both because of the time horizons involved and because new projects may involve operating in areas in which the company has no previous experience. Risk assessment is a vital part of capital investment appraisal, but coping with it purely by increasing the discount rate applied to a project is a crude and generally inadequate technique. Better accounting-based techniques for the assessment of risk and its impact need to be developed as a matter of urgency.

Capital budgeting is a unique blend of objective, quantitative measurement and subjective judgment. Both types of information have their part to play and the art of capital investment appraisal lies in blending objective, but inadequate, information with important but subjective information, to come to a balanced and reasoned decision.

PART THREE

Summary and prescriptions for practice

· 9 ·

Accounting for
effective control

Accounting information is a vital aid to control in most organizations. Budget systems provide a formal means of assisting in the
continual comparison that must take place between what is
desirable and what is possible. They can also provide the necessary
structure for setting effective motivational targets which can then act
as a standard against which actual performance is evaluated.
However, they do not and cannot provide a sufficient basis for the
overall control of an enterprise, which must rest on much broader
foundations. The effective use of accounting information requires a
balance to be achieved between all the various control techniques
that are available, both accounting and non-accounting.

This is no easy task. In many ways, large organizations appear to
be less than fully controllable, and the major role played by the
various control techniques is to tackle currently urgent problems,
and to rectify the immediate deficiencies that are apparent. Yet it
must also be recognized that over-control is as hazardous as lack of
control. In particular, there is a tendency for previous controls to
remain in place when new ones are introduced. But if too great an
emphasis is placed on the achievement of certain defined tasks,
equally important but less measurable aspects of the job may be
neglected. The role of the management control system is to ensure
that this delicate balance between particular controls is achieved, so
as to obtain effective overall control.

Because it serves this balancing function, the management control
system is unique among the wider range of controls, for it is

concerned with overall *control*, not just the imposition of *controls* (Drucker, 1964). Many different controls can be used to get particular tasks achieved, and it is often a matter of managerial choice which one is actually used. It is a matter of common observation that similar results are obtained in a variety of different ways by different organizations. However, there are very few mechanisms available for achieving coherent and effective overall organizational control. Here accounting information systems play a unique and vital role in measuring, reporting and evaluating both managerial and unit performance.

Nevertheless, despite the central importance of accounting information in the process of achieving overall organizational control, it is not of itself sufficient. Other information must be used to interpret and evaluate the accounting measurements that are made, particularly in assessing the longer-term aspects of performance evaluation. The art of accounting control lies in its careful application, so that it achieves what it is capable of achieving without harming other aspects of organizational activity.

Some conflicts in accounting information systems use

The achievement of this balance is not just an accounting activity. It depends primarily on the proper use of accounting information by senior managers and by their line subordinates, as well as on the design of an appropriate technical accounting system. The role of the accountant is thus two-fold. First, the accountant must design and tailor the accounting information system to meet the particular circumstances of the organization being controlled. Second, he/she must educate and support line managers to use the information provided in a sensible and appropriate manner. It is a sad fact that the formal education of most accountants neglects this second task, although some undoubtedly develop the necessary expertise in the course of their everyday work. One purpose of this book is to help alert accountants, both those already qualified and those currently in training, to some of the personal, behavioural and organizational issues involved in using accounting information for effective management control.

In one sense, the very power of accounting as a universal tool that is applicable to all organizations is its fundamental weakness. Because accounting information of any type can be made available, it may be produced and then used in quite inappropriate ways. Accounting systems are frequently transferred from one context to another as accountants change jobs in the course of developing their careers, and they take with them systems that have proved their worth in a particular set of circumstances. However, the results of transferring such systems do not always turn out as expected and, in adapting them to fit new circumstances, practising management accountants develop their expertise and understanding, informally constructing their own contingency theories of accounting systems design. Managers also transfer their ways of using accounting information both between organizations as they change jobs, and also between hierarchical levels as they are promoted. They, too, discover that skills which work effectively in one context are less effective in other contexts, and require to be adapted.

The potential for mismatch is thus two-fold. The technical accounting system may fit its organizational context less than perfectly; also the way in which it is used may not be entirely appropriate. The job of the management accountant is to produce the most technically adequate system that is possible, and then to educate managers to make the best use of the information it provides, while recognizing its inherent limitations.

The very generality of accounting information is a further problem. Accounting information is invariably used for a wide range of different purposes. Inevitably it is better suited to some of these purposes than to others. Yet, because of a widespread belief in the objectivity and reliability of accounting systems, the information they produce may often be confidently used in quite inappropriate ways. For example, just as full cost information can be misleading if used as a basis for short-term decision-making, so aggregates of motivational budget targets may not provide a sound basis for corporate planning. The development of knowledge about how best to use accounting information in various circumstances is an urgent priority in the education of both accountants and managers.

The trade-off that always has to be made is between an emphasis on that which is measurable in a quantitative and objective manner, and that which is less easily measured and which can only be presented in qualitative and subjective terms. For example, in a manufacturing company there is often a trade-off to be made between quantity of output and its quality, and between short-term performance and laying the foundations for longer-term efficiency. In a finance company the same basic conflict may be expressed as the trade-off between current new business obtained and the default rate subsequently experienced.

In both cases, the qualitative impact of such policy decisions on customers needs to be assessed. Although it is relatively easy to measure current results, too great an emphasis on current performance targets can lead to the neglect of the less quantifiable, but equally important longer-term aspects of performance.

This effect is particularly noticeable in the emphasis that is placed on financial controls when an organization faces a financial crisis. Here, short-term accounting figures such as cash flows quite rightly play a dominant role, for if the organization fails to survive in the short-term there will be no longer-term to consider. However, in more normal circumstances, a more even balance between short- and long-term controls needs to be maintained. This is a matter of fundamental corporate policy and needs careful deliberation and explicit communication throughout the organization. The way senior managers use accounting information, and the stress they lay on particular aspects of measured performance, will have a strong influence on the actions of their subordinates. Because junior managers may see their rewards as being contingent upon the achievement of good short-term results, it is all too easy for work aimed at building strong longer-term foundations to be neglected because its effectiveness is much more difficult to evaluate.

More recently, the widespread availability of computerized accounting systems has lead to a further problem. In such systems there is frequently a high degree of integration between financial and management accounting, with the same underlying database being used to generate both external financial reports and internal management accounting reports. Although this is desirable both for reasons of economy and comparability, it can be carried too far with the same *method* of accounting being used for quite different purposes. For example, the method of depreciation used for taxation purposes (and possibly for external reporting) may be quite unsuitable for calculations of profit or residual income used for divisional performance appraisal. There is no difficulty in designing a computerized system that can produce different sets of figures based on different principles for different purposes; indeed it is much simpler to do this on a computerized system than on a manual system. But, in practice, there is a tendency to use the same set of calculated figures for all purposes, with the inevitable result that the figures produced are not at all suitable for some of the purposes for which they are used.

What has been said so far may be seen as a somewhat gloomy depiction of the many ways in which it is possible to mis-use accounting information. This is not altogether out of place because it is only too easy to discover ways in which accounting information is misused in almost any organization. Yet to focus on misuse, although it is widespread, is misleading as it overlooks the many ways in which accounting information is found to be useful and helpful. Research studies of budgetary control over the years have also tended to concentrate on the dysfunctional and harmful behaviour that the inappropriate use of control systems can engender, and to overlook the many functional activities that all systems generate. However, the evidence of empirical surveys strongly suggests that accounting information systems have a vital role to play in organizational control.

Admittedly, such systems have to be used with care and understanding; for what powerful tool does not? But if care and attention is paid to avoiding the major pitfalls that have been reviewed in the preceding chapters, accounting information is an indispensable tool for the manager seeking to exercise effective overall control.

Accounting and organizational culture

Nevertheless, the role of culture and politics within the organization should not be understated. Organizations are not totally rational entities which relentlessly pursue economic rationality to the exclusion of all other factors. They are also conglomerations of individuals who bring with them their own beliefs, values, objectives and abilities. Further, the organization is set in a wider external environment and is thus subject to a variety of external pressures and influences. We do not fully understand the impact of these various forces on organizational functioning, but it is evident that they affect organizational activities in major ways. Indeed, the idea of manipulating corporate culture as a means of effective management has received widespread publicity of late, although the extent to which corporate culture is actually open to influence by managers is debatable.

Viewed from this wider context, it is evidently unrealistic to expect the accounting system to act as a major agent for organizational change. More plausibly it provides a means for helping consolidate changes which are occurring for more fundamental reasons. The installation of new budgetary procedures, or the implementation of new measures of managerial performance based on accounting information, are means of supporting changes introduced to achieve more general aims. For example, the recent moves in the UK towards privatization and the introduction of competition into public services has been accompanied by the development of appropriate accounting information systems as a necessary, but not sufficient, part of the process of change.

One major example is the introduction of general management and clinical budgeting into the British National Health Service. It is evident that the success of the budgeting exercise in the NHS will be dependent upon the success of the wider aim of introducing an effective management system, able to cope with the powerful vested interests inherent in the present structure. The accounting system and, more importantly, the associated accountability arrangements are part of the means being used to pursue the broader aim of more effective direction and control, and a shift in the balance of power away from the *providers* of services towards both the *consumers* of these services and the *taxpayers* who foot the bill.

This shift in power also requires a shift in strongly held beliefs and values by many of the individuals involved, and thus represents a major change in corporate culture. There is evidence to suggest that this change in culture has been less effectively managed than some of the more tangible aspects of the change. The new accounting systems will only be effective to the extent that the required shift in power occurs, although it should be recognized that the introduction of the new systems is itself one of the means that is being used to help effect the power shift.

Thus the design and use of accounting information systems is inevitably bound up in the wider processes of organizational change, which involve both culture (values) and politics (power). Although the accounting system can be used as one means to promote such change, changes in the accounting system alone are generally inadequate in generating effective organizational change. The use of accounting information influences organizational activities much less than it is influenced by them. The implication for the accounting systems designers is that they must be responsive to the wider environment in which they work, and mould their systems to fit in with the wider aims and strategies being pursued.

This perspective also throws light on the contingency theory of management accounting. It is relatively easy to accept that the major contingent variables proposed to date (e.g. environment, technology, organizational structure, corporate strategy, size, ownership) have an effect in determining the most appropriate accounting information system for an organization. However, contingency theory provides only a static view of accounting information systems (AIS) design, and may perhaps be seen as indicating the steady state towards which the AIS will evolve if the contingent factors remain unchanged. But, in the real world, change is a continual fact of organizational life, and further changes are likely to occur before the process of evolution is complete.

Thus, two scenarios are possible. First, AIS design may be continually catching up with external and internal changes or, in some cases, be ahead of them because it is being used to promote them. At any point in time, there will be an inevitable mismatch between the actual situation and the hypothesised ideal. Second, an organization may take a conscious decision not to change its AIS, despite the mismatch between the system and organizational needs; the advantages in maintaining a stable AIS may be thought to outweigh the disadvantages of having a less than perfect match. Thus, although contingency theory may be able to provide guidance to the AIS designer about the features of a good system in particular circumstances, in practice a mismatch will almost certainly be found.

To the extent that such issues are appreciated by practising managers and management accountants, their knowledge has usually been gained from practical experience rather than from theories of management or accounting. Traditional accounting textbooks consistently neglect to discuss such matters. Further, the professional education of accountants tends to concentrate solely upon matters of technical systems design rather than on issues of systems use and development. It is this gap between technical systems design and their use in practice by managers that this book tries to bridge. Inevitably, because our present state of knowledge is skimpy, only very general direction and advice can be given at this stage. Nevertheless, it is hoped that raising such issues as a matter for discussion and debate will allow futher progress to be made.

The aim of this book has been to set the design and use of an accounting information system into the wider context of overall organizational control in a changing environment, so that both managers and accountants can become better aware of the human and managerial issues involved. The effective use of accounting information is a vital managerial skill, and it is the management accountant who should be able to provide the necessary advice and guidance to the busy manager. The accounting information system is a powerful tool that needs to be used wisely and with regard to its inherent limitations. But, properly used, it is a vital weapon in the fight to achieve effective management control.

An accounting information systems check list

This chapter consists of a set of questions designed to assist both managers and accountants to appraise the effectiveness of the accounting information systems currently in use in their organizations. A thorough consideration of the issues raised by these questions will generate ideas for change, and also provide a means for evaluating the likely consequences of possible changes. However, it should be constantly borne in mind that accounting control systems interact with many other mechanisms of control, and it is the impact of the total range of controls adopted that is important.

Overall objectives

1 An AIS is a tool designed to assist in the achievement of overall organizational objectives. How does the AIS, and the ways in which it is used, fit into an overall scheme of control?

How is accounting control viewed in the context of overall corporate culture, and the subcultures of various parts of the organization?

2 How good a fit is the AIS with other organizational and environmental characteristics?

What are the most important contingencies faced, and what impact do (should) they have on AIS design?

How has the AIS evolved over the last few years, and is this evolution consistent with current corporate strategy?

3 To what extent is the AIS concerned with measuring, monitoring and controlling:
- Inputs into the conversion process?
- Outputs from the conversion process?
- The internal operation of the conversion process?
- The behaviour of individuals?

4 How does the AIS link with other systems in determining:
- What the dimensions of good performance are?
- How standards of performance are set?
- How actual performance is monitored?
- How rewards are linked to performance?

5 What role does the AIS play in:
- Strategic (corporate) planning?
- Business unit planning?
- Management control?
- Operational (task) control?

How are these roles linked, and how are conflicts resolved?

6 An AIS can be used either as a control from above, or as a means of providing information to enable individual managers to exercise control themselves. Is the way in which the AIS is used consistent with the major objective chosen?

Budgetary control

7 Budgets can serve a variety of purposes. Which of the following are the most imporant?
- Authorization and control of spending.
- Accurate forecasting of financial results.
- Planning financial requirements.
- Business unit planning.
- Operations planning.
- Communication of information and expectations.
- Coordination of activities.
- Motivation of improved performance.
- Evaluation of operating unit performance.
- Evaluation of managerial performance.

Which of these purposes should the budget be designed to serve?

Are different purposes served at different hierarchical levels? If so, how are differences to be reconciled? How will the chosen purposes interact with each other?

8 How does the budgetary control system relate to other controls used by managers?
   - Is some information redundant?
   - Should additional information be provided?
   - How does the accounting information relate to that provided by other management information systems?
9 How is the budgetary control system used by line managers?
   What rewards (both explicit and implicit) are connected with meeting the budget?
   How does this affect the accuracy of the information entered into the budget system (both budget standard and actual performance data)?

Specific issues

10 Are budgets intended to act as motivational targets? If so:
   - Are the targets set at the level of difficulty most appropriate to *each* manager? How can this be checked?
   - To what extent do managers participate in setting targets?
   - Are there too many targets? Too many difficult targets?
   - Is there adequate and timely feedback of results?
   - How are budget variances treated? Are managers allowed freedom to fail?
11 Are budgets used as a means of appraising performance? If so:
   - Are managerial and unit performance distinguished?
   - How well does the budget represent the performance that is desired?
   - How are budget standards set?
   - How is uncertainty allowed for?
   - Can the performance measure be improved by undesirable practices? Does this occur in practice?
   - Is actual performance misreported? How and why?
   - Is a balance maintained between short- and long-term performance? Between measurable and less measurable aspects of performance?
   - How do line managers use budget information?
   - How do they react to budget variances? Are allowances made for individual differences?
   - How fair do junior managers consider the system to be?

- To what extent do junior managers participate in budget formulation and revision?
12 Are budgets used as planning forecasts? If so:
   - How, and by whom, are budget standards set?
   - Have budgets been achieved in the past?
   - What is the distribution of past budget variances?
   - Can bias in budget estimates be corrected? How? Privately or by formal budget changes?
   - Should planning be uncoupled from budgetary control?
13 How is the capital budgeting process organized?
   - What is its relationship with operating budgeting?
   - How are investment opportunities identified?
   - How are expected cash flows estimated and audited?
   - How is risk and uncertainty taken into account?
   - What criteria are used in formal evaluation?
   - What mechanisms for post-audit exist?
   - How are potential conflicts between project appraisal and subsequent performance appraisal dealt with?

The budget process

14 Where does each item of budget information come from?
   - Who influences it?
   - How is it amended at each stage of budget formulation?
   - What is its final form and use?
15 Does the budget serve different purposes at different organizational levels? If so, how is it adapted to ensure that it is appropriate?
16 What mechanisms are used to handle budget aggregation? Are they appropriate to the uses made of budget information?
17 How well does the budget system:
   - Measure the value of scarce resources?
   - Predict the outcomes of planned activities?
   - Deal with complexity and interdependence?
   - Deal with uncertainty?
   - Assist in resolving conflicts?

The accounting information system

18 How well does the AIS fit the situations in which it is used? Can the contingency theory of management accounting be used to indicate any potential mismatches?

How consistent is the use made of accounting information with the professional, corporate and national cultures in which it is applied.

19 What impediments exist to the full use of accounting information? How can these be overcome?

20 To what extent do the accounting controls used promote effective overall management control?

21 Are any changes required? If so:
- Can the effects of the proposed changes be predicted?
- Can the changes be made incrementally?
- Is some training appropriate for managers? For accountants?
- Should further investigation and research be undertaken?
- Should specialist advice be sought?

Guide to
further reading

This book provides a general introduction to the use of accounting information in management control, and has concentrated on the human, behavioural and organizational aspects of accounting control. There is much else that has been written on the topic, so this chapter seeks to guide the interested reader into some of this wider literature. First, some books which give alternative general introductions are suggested, and the ways in which they supplement the present book are pointed out. Second, a small number of surveys is reviewed, the aim of which is to give a comprehensive overview of the current state of knowledge in the field. Finally, some books which will assist the reader in studying the source research literature, upon which most of what is written here is based, are suggested.

General books

Merchant, K. A., *Control in Business Organizations*, Pitman, 1985

This, the first book in the Pitman series on the role of accounting in organizations and society, is a highly readable overview of the various types of control mechanisms that are available to managers. Written for use on the Harvard MBA programme, it is short, jargon-free and packed with real-world examples. Its major chapters focus on results controls, action (behaviour) controls and personnel controls, with particular emphasis on how to make controls tighter or looser and the potential for harmful side-effects. It concludes with an extended discussion on the role of financial and accounting controls and the problem of overall control systems design. Although written primarily for managers rather than accountants, it provides an excellent introduction for accountants who wish to consider the broader issues of management control in a very practical way.

Hopwood, A. G., *Accounting and Human Behaviour*, Prentice-Hall, 1976.

Although becoming slightly dated, this is an easily read account of the various ways in which accounting information can be used to affect human behaviour. The first part of the book is concerned with budgetary control and the role of accounting data in performance evaluation. Later chapters consider the use of information in decision-making and the impact of external financial reports, before a concluding discussion on accounting systems design. There have been considerable advances made in the ten years since this book was published, but it remains a useful introduction to the topic.

Emmanuel, C. R. and Otley, D. T., *Accounting for Management Control*, Van Nostrand Reinhold, 1985.

Written primarily for undergraduate accounting students, the first part of the text covers much of the background material to issues dealt with in the present book. However, in its second and third parts it goes into much more detail about how to design accounting information systems that are appropriate to particular organizational circumstances. It argues that traditional accounting techniques were designed to suit relatively simple, centralized organizations operating in stable environments. The third part therefore concentrates on the design of accounting control systems for complex, divisionalized organizations operating in conditions of considerable uncertainty. A useful book for those who require more accounting detail than is presented here.

Dermer, J., *Management Planning and Control Systems*, Irwin, 1977.

This text provides a general overview of the design of management planning and control systems and contains a large number of case study examples. The strength of the book is the way in which it links accounting systems design with the more general issues of organizational design and strategic planning. It contains an excellent account of the overall strategic planning process and how it links with management control. Finally, it develops a contingency framework for situational systems design for both the organization as a whole and for individual responsibility centres. This is a book which combines theoretical insights with sound practical applications.

Mintzberg, H., *Impediments to the Use of Accounting Information*, National Association of Accountants, 1975.

A brief report written for the US National Association of Accountants and the Society of Industrial Accountants of Canada, which provides the full ten-point analysis (outlined in Chapter 6 of this book) of why accounting information may not be used effectively. Three major areas of concern are identified: formal v informal information conflicts; organizational problems; and individual cognitive problems. Several recommendations are made including the need to develop broader-based information systems, intelligent filtering mechanisms, and systems having the capability for in-depth search. More controversially, it also suggests the possibility of information systems containing multiple, conflicting sources of data on the grounds that managers need different points of view and contrary opinions to counterbalance their own prejudices. Highly reccommended reading for all those concerned with AIS design.

Handy, C., *Understanding Organizations* (3rd ed), Penguin, 1985.

Although containing little material specifically about accounting systems, this is a practical and managerial approach to applying the basic concepts of social psychology and organization theory to problems of management control. The first part of the book develops the basic concepts of motivation, roles, power, groups, culture and politics and the second part applies these to organizational issues and problems. The text is full of inset boxes containing a variety of interesting and apposite illustrations of the theoretical concepts. The book is particularly strong on the role of culture in organizational control, and provides an excellent introduction to organization theory for those with little prior exposure to the subject.

Surveys

Hofstede, G., *The Game of Budget Control*, Tavistock, 1968.

Despite being based on studies carried out in 1964–65, this remains one of the more comprehensive studies of the operation of budgetary control systems that is available. But, more importantly, the first four chapters survey the literature available at that time, and the final chapters contain useful practical recommendations and suggested directions for future research. A classic book, representing a milestone in the development of AIS research, and essential reading for those who wish to gain an appreciation of how the subject has developed.

Scapens, R. W., Otley, D. T., and Lister, R. J., *Management Accounting, Organizational Theory and Capital Budgeting: Three Surveys*, Macmillan/ESRC, 1984.

These three surveys are a comprehensive review of the state-of-the-art of management accounting research up to about 1983. Scapens surveys developments in mainstream management accounting research over the last twenty years; Otley reviews the application of concepts and ideas from organization theory to management accounting; and Lister outlines the current state of capital budgeting theory and its links with finance theory more generally. Together the three surveys represent an invaluable account of most of the research work undertaken in management accounting over the past two decades, and are essential reading for serious researchers in the field. They are also readable enough to allow the general reader to get a good picture of these developments.

Livingstone, J. L. and Ferris, K. R. (eds), *Management Planning and Control: The Behavioral Foundations*, Century VII Publishing Co., 1987.

This book contains a dozen invited articles that review most of the major areas in management accounting and control from a behavioural point of view. They are written at an introductory level, but are authored by some of the leading researchers in the field, and thus provide an authoritative summary of the current state-of-the-art for the non-specialist reader. It contains sections on organizational strategy, divisional planning and control, the measurement of business unit performance, budgetary control and managerial decision-making. The best introductory summary available.

Research literature

Macintosh, N. B., *The Social Software of Accounting Information Systems*, Wiley, 1985.

This book provides a comprehensive introduction to the research literature on behavioural aspects of AIS design. Most of the text consists of summaries of the findings of recent research, presented in a much more comprehensible way than the original articles. As the title indicates, the book is concerned with the use of accounting and other management information in its human, social and organizational context. A brave attempt is made to present the studies in a theoretically coherent manner, although this is only partly successful due to the diversity of the subject matter. The book concludes with the author's own technological model of management control systems. It represents the best available introduction to the modern research literature on the subject.

Lowe, T. and Machin, J. L. J., *New Perspectives in Management Control*, Macmillan, 1983.

An attempt to codify the underlying theory of the design and operation of management control systems, this book contains fourteen contributed chapters. However, each chapter was reviewed by other contributors and revised before publication, giving a more coherent sense of purpose than exists in most collections of separately authored chapters. Overall it represents a broad insight into management control systems design, drawing eclectically from a wide range of academic disciplines including economics, the behavioural sciences, accounting, cybernetics, general systems theory and management and administrative theory.

Chenhall, R. H., Harrison, G. L. and Watson, D. J. H., *The Organizational Context of Management Accounting*. Pitman, 1981.

This is a collection of reprinted articles from the major research journals, designed to indicate the flavour of the work being undertaken in the 1970s. A strength of the collection is the substantial text which is interleaved between the articles. This introduces each piece and tries to set it in its context and assess its significance. The collection thus provides a relatively easy means of making the transition from books which summarize research studies to the research literature itself, and will be of value to those who wish to progress to reading original articles.

Accounting, Organizations and Society, Pergammon Press.

Although relevant material is published in a wide range of accounting and management journals. *Accounting, Organizations and Society* is the journal which specializes in material concerned with the interrelationship between accounting, its use in organizations, and its wider societal impact. Written for academics, its articles require sustained concentration to read, but can prove highly rewarding for the insights they contain.

References

Ackerman, R. W., 'Influence of Integration and Diversity on the Investment Process', *Administrative Science Quarterly*, 1970, pp. 341–52.

Aharoni, Y., *The Foreign Investment Decision Process*, (Boston, Harvard Graduate School of Business, 1966).

Amey, L. R. and Egginton D., *Management Accounting: A Conceptual Approach*, (London, Longman, 1973).

Anthony, R. N., *Planning and Control Systems: A Framework for Analysis*, (Boston, Harvard Graduate School of Business, 1965).

Argyris, C., *The Impact of Budgets on People*, (Ithaca, NY, The Controllership Foundation, 1952).

Baumler, J. V., 'Defined Criteria of Performance in Organizational Control', *Administrative Science Quarterly*, 1971, pp. 340–9.

Benbasat, I. and Dexter, A. S., 'Value and Events Approaches to Accounting: An Experimental Evaluation', *The Accounting Review*, 1979, pp. 735–49.

Berg, N. A., 'Strategic planning in conglomerate companies', *Harvard Business Review*, May/June 1965, pp. 79–92.

Bower, J. L., *Managing the Resource Allocation Process*, (Boston, Harvard Graduate School of Business, 1971).

Brownell, P., 'Participation in Budgeting, Locus of Control and Organizational Effectiveness', *The Accounting Review*, October 1981, pp. 844–60.

Burgoyne, J. G., 'Stress, Motivation and Learning', in Gowler, D. and Legge, K. (eds), *Managerial Stress*, (Gower, 1975).

Caroll, S. and Tosi, H., *Management by Objectives: Applications and Research*, (New York, Macmillan, 1973).

Carter, E. E., 'The Behavioural Theory of the Firm and Top Level Corporate Decisions', *Administrative Science Quarterly*, 1971, pp. 413–28.

Cyert, R. M., March, J. G., and Starbuck, W. H., 'Two Experiments on Risk and Conflict in Organizational Estimation', *Management Science*, 1961, pp. 254–64.

Dew, R. B. and Gee, K. P., *Management Control and Information*, (London, Macmillan, 1973).

Doctor, R. H. and Hamilton, W. F., 'Cognitive Style and the Acceptance of Management Science Recommendations', *Management Science*, 1973, pp. 884–94.

Drucker, P. 'Control, Controls and Management', in Bonini, C. P. (ed.), *Management Controls: New Directions in Basic Research*, (New York, McGraw-Hill, 1964).

Edey, H. C., *Business Budgets and Accounts* (3rd ed.) (London, Hutchinson, 1966).

Emmanuel, C. R., and Otley, D. T., 'The Usefulness of Residual Income', *Journal of Business Finance and Accounting*, 1976, pp. 43–51.

Emmanuel, C. R., and Otley, D. T., *Accounting for Management Control* (London, Van Nostrand Reinhold, 1985).

Gilbert, T. F., *Human Competence: Engineering Worthy Performance* (New York, McGraw-Hill, 1978).

Gordon, L. A. and Miller, D., 'A Contingency Framework for the Design of Accounting Information Systems, *Accounting, Organizations and Society*, 1976, pp. 59–70.

Govindarajan, V., 'Apropriateness of Accounting Data in Performance Evaluation: An Empirical Evaluation of Environmental Uncertainty as an Intervening Variable', *Accounting, Organizations and Society*, 1984, pp. 125–36.

Henderson, B. D. and Dearden, J., 'New System for Divisional Control', *Harvard Business Review*, Sept/Oct, 1966, pp. 144–60.

Hertz, D. B., 'Risk Analysis in Capital Investment', *Harvard Business Review*, Jan/Feb 1964, pp. 175–86.

Hirst, M. K., 'Accounting Information and the Evaluation of Subordinate Performance', *The Accounting Review*, 1981, pp. 771–84.

Hofstede, G., *The Game of Budget Control*, (London, Tavistock, 1968).

Hopwood, A. G., 'An Empirical Study of the Role of Accounting Data in Performance Evaluation', *Empirical Research in Accounting, Supplement to Journal of Accounting Research*, 1972, pp. 156–82.

Ivancevich, J. 'Effects of Goal-Setting on Performance and Job Satisfaction', *Journal of Applied Psychology*, 1976, pp. 605–12.

Jaques, E., *Equitable Payment*, (London, Heinemann, 1961).

Jones, C. S., 'An Empirical Study of the Role of Management Accounting Systems Following Takeover or Merger', *Accounting, Organizations and Society*, 1985, pp. 303–28.

Kenis, I., 'Effects of Budgetary Goal Characteristics on Managerial Attitudes and Performance', *The Accounting Review*, 1979, pp. 707–21.

King, P. 'Is the Emphasis of Capital Budgeting Theory Misplaced?', *Journal of Business Finance and Accounting*, 1975, pp. 69–82.

Klammer, T., 'The Association of Capital Budgeting Techniques with Firm Performance', *The Accounting Review*, 1973, pp. 387–97.

Lawler, E. E., *Motivation in Work Organizations*, (Wadsworth, 1973).

Lister, R. J., 'Capital Budgeting: A Survey', in Scapens, R. W., Otley, D. T. and Lister, R. J., *op. cit.*, 1984.

Locke, E. A., 'Towards a Theory of Task Motivation and Incentives', *Organizational Behaviour and Human Performance*, 1968, pp. 157–89.

Lowe, E. A., 'Budgetary Control: An Evaluation in a Wider, Managerial Perspective', *Accountancy*, November 1970, pp. 764–9.

Lowe, E. A. and Shaw, R. W., 'An Analysis of Managerial Biasing: Evidence from a Company's Budgeting Process', *Journal of Management Studies*, 1968, pp. 304–15.

Lowe, T. and Machin, J. L. J., (eds), *New Perspectives in Management Control*, (London, Macmillan, 1983).

Machin, J. L. J., 'Management Control Systems: Whence and Whither?', pp. 22–42 in Lowe, T. and Machin, J. L. J., (eds), *op. cit.* 1983.

Macintosh, N. B., *The Social Software of Accounting and Information Systems* (New York, Wiley, 1985).

Merchant, K. A., 'The Design of the Corporate Budgeting System: Influences on Managerial Behaviour and Performance', *The Accounting Review*, 1981, pp. 813–29.

Meyer, H. H., Kay, E. and French J. R. P., 'Split Roles in Performance Appraisal', *Harvard Business Review*, Jan./Feb. 1965, pp.123–29.

Milani, K., 'The Relationship of Participation in Budget-Setting to Industrial Supervisor Performance and Attitudes: A Field Study', *The Accounting Review*, 1975, pp. 274–83.

Mintzberg, H., *Impediments to the Use of Management Information* (New York, National Association of Accountants, 1975).

Otley, D. T., 'Budget Use and Managerial Performance', *Journal of Accounting Research*, 1978, pp. 122–49.

Otley, D. T., 'The Contingency Theory of Management Accounting: Achievement and Prognosis', *Accounting, Organizations and Society*, 1980, pp. 413–28.

Otley, D. T., 'Management Accounting and Organization Theory: A Review of their Interrelationship', pp. 96–164 in Scapens, R. W., Otley, D. T. and Lister, R. J., *Management Accounting, Organizational Theory and Capital Budgeting: Three Surveys* (London, Macmillan/ESRC, 1984).

Otley, D. T., 'Bias in Budget Estimates: Some Statistical Evidence, *Journal of Business Finance and Accounting*, 1985, pp. 415–28.

Otley, D. T. and Berry, A. J., 'Risk Distribution in the Budgetary Process', *Accounting and Business Research*, 1979, pp. 325–37.

Otley, D. T. and Berry, A. J., 'Control, Organization and Accounting', *Accounting, Organizations and Society*, 1980, pp. 231–46.

Otley, D. T. and Dias, F. B. J., 'Accounting Aggregation and Decision-Making Performance: An Experimental Investigation', *Journal of Accounting Research*, 1982, pp. 171–88.

Ouchi, W. G., 'A Conceptual Framework for the Design of Organizational Control Mechanisms', *Management Science*, 1979, pp. 833–48.

Pinches, G. E., 'Myopia, Capital Budgeting and Decision-Making', *Financial Management*, 1982, pp. 6–19.

Prakash, P. and Rappaport, A. 'Information Inductance and its Significance for Accounting', *Accounting, Organizations and Society*, 1977, pp. 29–38.

Ridgway, V. F., 'Dysfunctional Consequences of Performance Measurements', *Administrative Science Quarterly*, 1956, pp. 240–47.

Sathe, V., 'The Relevance of Modern Organization Theory for Managerial Accounting', *Accounting, Organizations and Society*, 1978, pp. 89–92.

Scapens, R. W., Sale, J. T. and Tikkas, P. A., *Controlling Divisional Capital Expenditure* (London, ICMA, 1982).

Scapens, R. W., Otley, D. T. and Lister, R. J., *Management Accounting, Organization Theory and Capital Budgeting: Three Surveys* (London, ESRC/Macmillan, 1984).

Schiff, M. and Lewin, A. Y., 'The Impact of People on Budgets', *The Accounting Review*, 1970, pp. 259–68.

Sherwood, D., *Financial Modelling: A Practical Guide* (London, Gee & Co., 1983).

Solomons, D., *Divisional Performance: Measurement and Control* (Homewood, Ill., Irwin, 1965).

Stedry, A. C., *Budget Control and Cost Behaviour*, (Englewood Cliffs, N. J., Prentice-Hall, 1960).

Stedry, A. C. and Kay, E., The Effects of Goal Difficulty on Performance', *Behavioral Science*, 1966, pp. 459–70.

Steers, R. M., *Organizational Effectiveness: A Behavioral View* (Santa Monica, Ca., Goodyear, 1977).

Thomas, A. L., 'Transfer Prices of the Multinational Firm: When will they be Arbitary?', *Abacus*, 1971, pp. 40–53.

Thompson, J. D., *Organizations in Action* (McGraw-Hill, 1967).

Tosi, H., 'The Human Effects of Managerial Budgeting Systems', in Livingstone, J. L. (ed.), *Management Accounting: The Behavioral Foundations* (Columbus, Ohio, Grid, 1975).

Wildavsky, A., *Budgeting: A Comparative Theory of the Budgeting Process* (Boston, Little, Brown, 1975).

Williamson, O. E., *The Economics of Discretionary Behavior* (Englewood Cliffs, N. J., Prentice-Hall 1964).

Williamson, O. E., *Corporate Control and Business Behavior* (Englewood Cliffs, N. J., Prentice-Hall, 1970).

Index

Author

Subject